## Praise for *Cursed in New England*

"Joe Citro writes the best and most believable stories about the supernatural since Edgar Allan Poe. *Cursed in New England* is especially engaging because in it, Mr. Citro brings his own wise and often hilarious personal interpretations to the wonderful tales he tells of accursed farms, mountains, graveyards, towns, houses, and families in a New England few tourists have ever visited. *Cursed in New England* is a splendid combination of off-beat social history, masterful storytelling, and absolutely first-rate writing from a true New England original with a life-long passion for things that go bump in the night and, come to think of it, in broad daylight, as well."

—Howard Frank Mosher, author of *Waiting for Teddy Williams*

"*Cursed in New England* is a must read. By gathering together stories, synthesizing them, and analyzing them, Joseph A. Citro has over the years made a significant contribution to New England history and culture. He does it all in a simple, elegant prose style and with insight and a sneaky sense of humor."

—Ernest Hebert, author of *The Old American,* *The Dogs of March,* and five other novels

*Steal not this Book my honest Friend*
*For fear the Gallows should be your end,*
*And when you die the Lord will say*
*And where's the Book you stole away?*

–Traditional book curse

# Books by Joseph A. Citro

Deus-X: The Reality Conspiracy (2003)

Curious New England (2003)

Vermont Air (2002)

Lake Monsters (2001)

The Gore (2000)

The Vermont Ghost Guide (2000)

Guardian Angels (1999)

Green Mountains, Dark Tales (1999)

Shadow Child (1998)

Passing Strange (1996)

Green Mountain Ghosts (1994)

Vermont Lifer (1986)

Learn more about Joseph A. Citro's books at
www.josephacitro.blogspot.com

# CURSED IN NEW ENGLAND

## MORE STORIES OF DAMNED YANKEES

Joseph A. Citro

*Illustrations by Jeff White*

**Globe
Pequot**

Guilford, Connecticut

## Globe
# Pequot

An imprint of The Rowman & Littlefield Publishing Group, Inc.
4501 Forbes Blvd., Ste. 200
Lanham, MD 20706
www.rowman.com

Distributed by NATIONAL BOOK NETWORK

First Globe Pequot edition, 2004.
This Globe Pequot paperback edition, 2018.

Illustrations by Jeff White

British Library Cataloguing in Publication Information available

The Library of Congress has previously catalogued an earlier paperback edition as follows:
Citro, Joseph A.
    Cursed in New England: stories of damned Yankees / Joseph A. Citro.–
1st ed. p. cm.
    Includes bibliographical references (p. ) and index.
    ISBN 0-7627-2868-X
    1. Blessing and cursing–New England–History. I. Title.

BF1558.C55 2004
133.4'4–dc22

ISBN 978-1-4930-3224-2 (paperback)
ISBN 978-1-4930-3221-1 (e-book)

Printed in the United States of America

This book is intended solely for the entertainment of its readers. The conjectures and opinions expressed herein are those of the author, and the publisher disclaims any responsibility for them.

It is a delicate matter to dedicate a book about curses.
With that in mind, this one is for that damned Bates,
who inspires more curses than anyone I know.

# CONTENTS

Preface . . . . . . . . . . . . . . . . . . . . . . . . . . . . . . . . . . . . . . . . . . . . . . . . x

Damned Yankees: An Introduction . . . . . . . . . . . . . . . . . . . . . . . . . . . 1

"A Dreadful Wizard" . . . . . . . . . . . . . . . . . . . . . . . . . . . . . . . . . . . . 15

The Burton Ail . . . . . . . . . . . . . . . . . . . . . . . . . . . . . . . . . . . . . . . . . 27

The Saga of the Saco River . . . . . . . . . . . . . . . . . . . . . . . . . . . . . . . . 37

A Blighted Campaign . . . . . . . . . . . . . . . . . . . . . . . . . . . . . . . . . . . . 47

The Phantom Foot . . . . . . . . . . . . . . . . . . . . . . . . . . . . . . . . . . . . . . 61

The Missing Man . . . . . . . . . . . . . . . . . . . . . . . . . . . . . . . . . . . . . . . 69

Connecticut's Village of the Damned . . . . . . . . . . . . . . . . . . . . . . . . . 83

Nix's Mate . . . . . . . . . . . . . . . . . . . . . . . . . . . . . . . . . . . . . . . . . . . . 99

That Old Sand Farm . . . . . . . . . . . . . . . . . . . . . . . . . . . . . . . . . . . . 107

No Mercy from Mercie Dale . . . . . . . . . . . . . . . . . . . . . . . . . . . . . . . 113

Fate and the *Phoenix* . . . . . . . . . . . . . . . . . . . . . . . . . . . . . . . . . . . 127

The Witch and the Virgin . . . . . . . . . . . . . . . . . . . . . . . . . . . . . . . . . 137

The Tree of Knowledge . . . . . . . . . . . . . . . . . . . . . . . . . . . . . . . . . . 153

An Idol Revenge . . . . . . . . . . . . . . . . . . . . . . . . . . . . . . . . . . . . . . . 161

Haunted Waters . . . . . . . . . . . . . . . . . . . . . . . . . . . . . . . . . . . . . . . 171

A Shadow Over Crompton . . . . . . . . . . . . . . . . . . . . . . . . . . . . . . . . 189

The Crash of Camelot . . . . . . . . . . . . . . . . . . . . . . . . . . . . . . . . . . . 199

A Cluster of Curses: An Epilogue . . . . . . . . . . . . . . . . . . . . . . . . . . . 215

Appendix: A Portion of an Anglican
  "Commination Service" . . . . . . . . . . . . . . . . . . . . . . . . . . . . . . . . . 235

Sources . . . . . . . . . . . . . . . . . . . . . . . . . . . . . . . . . . . . . . . . . . . . . . 237

Acknowledgments . . . . . . . . . . . . . . . . . . . . . . . . . . . . . . . . . . . . . . 256

Index . . . . . . . . . . . . . . . . . . . . . . . . . . . . . . . . . . . . . . . . . . . . . . . . 257

About the Author . . . . . . . . . . . . . . . . . . . . . . . . . . . . . . . . . . . . . . 262

About the Illustrator . . . . . . . . . . . . . . . . . . . . . . . . . . . . . . . . . . . . 262

# PREFACE

No one thinks very much about curses. Scientists don't study them. Forteans don't write about them. Psychic investigators don't test for them. If acknowledged at all, they're relegated to the province of the professional folklorist, yet even there they are rarely chronicled with any degree of seriousness.

But here in New England we are no strangers to curses, jinxes, imprecations, maledictions, execrations, whammies, whatever you want to call them. They've been with us for a long, long time—just as they have been a part of every culture on this earth.

To the unbeliever, there is no such thing. To believers, they are something to be feared. And to those who know, there's no hope of escape . . .

—J.A.C.
Burlington, Vermont
February 2004

# DAMNED YANKEES:
## AN INTRODUCTION

*Death will slay with its wings whoever disturbs the peace of
the pharaoh.*

–Alleged inscription on King Tut's Tomb

## AN UNHOLY ARSENAL

New Englanders curse all the time. But profane sputtering
by some crusty old Yankee is usually more humorous
than menacing.

Still, genuine maledictions–the opposite of benedictions–
have frequently been uttered on New England soil. These are
true curses, intended to invoke evil, injury, or total destruction
against an individual, a group, or possibly a whole family.
Curses laid against families have tormented succeeding generations, sometimes bringing death to the heirs, until an entire
line becomes extinct.

Such blasphemous condemnation has long been part of the
weaponry wielded by witches, priests, magicians, shamans, and
sometimes even ordinary civilian ill-wishers.

Curses are evident in almost every culture. They have been
used politically, as in the hands of Haiti's Papa Doc Duvalier.
They've been used for religious retribution, as in the terrifying
"Rod of Light" occasionally invoked by certain orthodox Jewish
sects.

As recently as 1981 Rabbi Moshe Hirsch threatened to call down "The Rod" to stop archaeologist Yigal Shilo from excavating the biblical city of David.

Even the Anglican Church has its commination service, containing twelve curses intended to be uttered in the house of God. It first appeared in *The Book of Common Prayer* in 1662. (See the appendix.)

And the Roman Catholics, with their excommunication ritual, condemn the targeted individual "to eternal fire with Satan and his angels," symbolically removing him or her from the sight of God and all possibility of redemption.

In this case the results of the curse may not be experienced until a person enters the afterlife. But for the purposes of this book, we're interested in what goes on here, in this world. So the mysteries we'll contemplate are restricted to two simple questions:

Is there evidence that curses work in this life?

And perhaps more thematically relevant: Do curses work in New England?

Both answers seem to be *yes*.

And why not? The New England region was founded by pious, fire-and-brimstone Christians. And Christianity itself is alleged to have begun with God's curse against Satan in retaliation for his temptation of Adam and Eve—not to mention His specific imprecations against all other participants: (1) the serpent, who was condemned to crawl on his belly; (2) all women, who would forever after suffer pain in childbirth and be subject to the authority of their husbands; (3) all men, who would eternally represent humanity cut off from the tree of life; and (4) the ground itself, which was cursed with thorns and thistles so man will have to toil mightily simply to produce sustenance enough to survive until the day he dies.

Or at least that's what our forefathers (and mothers) regarded as true.

The fact is, the Christian Bible is full of curses, from Genesis to Revelation. So it would seem that curses are more firmly rooted in our belief systems than we like to think. Our twenty-first-century intellects may reject them as primitive superstition, but somewhere in the atavistic composition of our souls, remnants of belief seem to survive.

Before the Europeans arrived, Native American stewards of the land had their own arsenal of curses. They directed them at each other, often with devastating results. Then—as we'll soon see—they turned their supernatural artillery against the Puritan invaders. Some of those maledictions reverberate to this day.

But of course the European interlopers brought with them their own propensity for preternatural warfare. Stories of damned and damning Yankees are legion. Each New England state provides its greater- and lesser-known favorites.

Many of those venerable Yankee curses are gathered here, in book form, for the first time.

## BLACK AGNES

My own interest in curses began where, most likely, everyone's begins: hearing the story of the deaths following the opening of King Tut's Tomb.

Allegedly, when Lord Carnarvon and Howard Carter opened Tutankhamen's tomb, a curse was set in motion. Subsequently, six of the seven-member excavation team died strange, sudden deaths. Lord Carnarvon himself was felled by a mosquito bite.

The episode is dramatic and convincing, especially if it's not studied too carefully. But it also happened a long time ago—1922—and half a world away, so to New Englanders there is a built-in sense of immunity.

My interest intensified soon afterward when I learned there are active curses much closer to home. Right here in my native Vermont. Almost underfoot and therefore way too close for comfort.

One of my earliest discoveries was the so-called Curse of Black Agnes in Montpelier, Vermont's capital city, within easy driving distance from my home.

The first version I heard of this frightening graveyard tale had to do with a Montpelierite who died around 1930, the victim of a murder.

An elegant monument was erected for him, adorned with a dark bronze statue of the Virgin Mary. She's cloaked, seated on a granite bench, with her sorrow-filled face upturned toward Heaven. Somewhere along—for reasons as yet inexplicable—she picked up the nickname Black Agnes.

It is widely believed that this elaborate gravestone is the instrument of a curse, for it is said that anyone who sits on Black Agnes's lap by the light of the full moon will suffer seven years of bad luck during which he or she might well die. No one, it is said, survives the seven years unscathed.

A number of "evidential anecdotes" back this up, usually articulated in the hushed tones of teenagers, often around a campfire, and all designed to illustrate that the curse really works.

One example has to do with a local high school boy's rite of passage. Supposedly he blatantly defied the curse by plunking himself down on Black Agnes's lap. Shortly afterward—and well within the fatal seven years—he drowned in a canoeing accident on the Winooski River. His bloated corpse was recovered less than half a mile from the fatal lap.

Since hearing this sinister saga, I have asked a number of people around Montpelier if they've ever sat on Black Agnes's lap. I couldn't find anyone who had, but plenty assured me they had not.

Upon inspection and investigation I discovered a few problems with the story. First and perhaps most conspicuous, the statue is not of the Virgin Mary at all. And it isn't any "Agnes," either. The anatomy is most distinctly male.

Interred beneath it is John E. Hubbard, a local philanthropist. Though his reputation was questioned for a time, and he had many enemies, he died of natural causes, not murder.

And his passing occurred in 1899, not "around 1930."

One wonders how his 5-foot-high bronze monument—created by artist Karl Bitter—ever earned such a tarnished reputation.

The "bad luck," the "full moon," and the "seven years" are all stock accoutrements of scary campfire tales and urban legends; they have little to do with legitimate curses.

The only suspenseful hint I was able to discover was that when Karl Bitter exhibited his prototype for the Hubbard monument at the 1904 World's Fair, he called it *Thanatos*, the Greek personification of death. So I suppose sitting on the "lap of death" might be a bit risky. But in truth, as far as I have been able to learn, no one has ever died within seven years of sitting on it. What's more, no one—as far as I can tell—has ever sat on it.

And nowhere in Montpelier is the statue identified by its Greek name. It is so anonymous and androgynous that to this day the bronze male effigy is routinely confused with the Virgin Mary.

## AMONG THE WITCHES

So my first New England curse story turned out to be bogus. I should have known. The mischief attributed to Black Agnes was too haphazard, too random. Ultimately lacking in logic. Curses are never directed without motive at incidental, innocent victims.

In fact, curses seem to fall into sensibly defined, somewhat logical categories:

1. Those intended to protect the weak from the strong, the powerless from the powerful.

2. Those intended to protect *things* such as property, jewels, books, or graves. We see King Tut's curse at work here. Even Shakespeare tried "Curse Insurance" to guard his corpse. On his tomb is written:

> GOOD FRIEND, FOR JESUS SAKE FORBEARE
> TO DIGGE THE DUST ENCLOASED HEARE.
> BLESTE BE YE MAN [THAT] SPARES THESE STONES,
> AND CURSTE BE HE [THAT] MOVES MY BONES.
> —William Shakespeare 1564–1616

3. And finally, there's the dreaded deathbed curse. The supercharged business of getting the ultimate last word was—and may still be—especially feared. All the curser's remaining psychic energy charges the curse, making it enormously potent. And revenge called down at the point of death is impossible to reverse. After all, there can be no reasoning, bargaining, or compromise after the light of life is forever extinguished.

## LAWS OF SUPERNATURE

With Black Agnes thoroughly and satisfactorily debunked, I went on to discover many other New England curses that could not be as easily dismissed. They conform to the "rules" of curses, and their stories make up the substance of this book.

Many cluster around the era of the witchcraft debacle of 1692 Salem, Massachusetts. Certainly there was a lot of evil afoot in those days, but its source may not have been satanic.

One of my favorite stories has to do with the time the young female "witch-spotters" from Salem were sent to the neighboring fishing village of Marblehead to ferret out any witches who might be residing there.

Marblehead was always an odd sort of place (one later embraced by H. P. Lovecraft in his fiction—but under an alias; he called it Kingsport), and old Wilmot "Mammy" Reed must have been an odd sort of woman. Apparently she was well known to the locals as a witch and had never made any bones about it. In early 1692, in front of many witnesses, she cursed Mrs. Simms of Salem, declaring that Goody Simms "would never mingere or carcare again." What's weird is that the increasingly uncomfortable Goody Simms was completely unable to urinate or defecate until September 22, 1692, the day Mammy Reed swung from a rope at Salem's Gallows Hill.

To the modern reader this story suggests the victim has a certain complicity in a curse's success. If Goody Simms hadn't believed that Mammy Reed was a witch and acknowledged her authority, perhaps the cursed constipation never would have occurred.

Conditioning and belief may indeed contribute to a curse's success. If victims know they have been targeted, and believe irrevocable doom is sure to follow, the victims probably do assist in their own demise. If that is true, it is logical that a curse would not affect an unbeliever.

But certain arguments refute this.

Some occultists maintain a curse is equally effective without the victim's knowledge. After all, if victims don't know they've been subjected to a curse, they can't seek assistance in removing it.

## MORE MASSACHUSETTS MALEDICTIONS

In Sutton, Massachusetts, the Widow Wakefield was an acknowledged cat lover and witch (the two often went hand in paw).

Goody Wakefield lived in a ramshackle house by the river. In order to feed her twenty cats, and herself, she went fishing every day for pickerel. As if to emphasize her eccentricity, she always appeared in the same outfit, winter or summer: a heavy coat with large pockets where she'd store her daily catch. As folklorist Robert Cahill writes, "Neither the evil eye nor the malignant touch was needed by Widow Wakefield to cast a spell, just to walk by her house or to pass her on the road would send one reeling from the smell."

One day two young Sutton lads decided to do the town a favor and get rid of the smelly old witch once and for all. Their mode of exorcism was to kill off her brood of familiars—her twenty cats.

Concealed by darkness, they managed to capture and execute seventeen of the Wakefield felines. Then they piled the broken bodies on a large rock in front of the "witch's" house so she'd see them first thing in the morning. No doubt they thought the appalling sight would instantly kill the old woman, or at least drive her away. If so, they thoroughly underestimated the Widow Wakefield. Instead, she concentrated the full force of her response in her powerful voice, shouting for all to hear, "God, curse these killers." She screamed it over and over again.

Within the year one of the young men drowned in the river and the other contracted an unknown disease that diminished his reason, ultimately leaving him a babbling idiot for the remainder of his days.

Those who heard the curse—as well as the reader—may be surprised that the Widow Wakefield had called on God and not the Devil.

But a curse is after all a prayer, and its author is no doubt tempted to summon the highest supernatural authority that is likely to cooperate. In this case the power of a known witch, reinforced by that of the Almighty, proved lethal medicine indeed.

## HISTORICAL HORROR

My very favorite witch tale is an irrefutable matter of history. It is also one of the most terrifying curses to be issued from the gallows in Salem, Massachusetts.

Its source was a condemned beggar named Sarah Good. But an examination of the downward spiral of her life might suggest Sarah herself was the one who had been cursed.

Though she had been born into a prosperous family, Sarah and her sisters were cheated out of their inheritance after her father's suicide in 1672.

Suddenly penniless, she married an equally impoverished suitor, an indentured servant named Daniel Poole. But Sarah's luck didn't improve; her new husband died shortly afterward. All she inherited was her husband's debts. Under Massachusetts law her second husband, William Good, was responsible for paying them off. But as a weaver and laborer, he couldn't. By 1689 he had to forfeit all his land and cattle to his creditors.

Sarah and William were reduced to begging. They lived in barns and sometimes in ditches. Sarah had a difficult time adjusting to her diminished stature and readily let her neighbors know they didn't meet her standards for "Christian charity." When she felt she had been slighted, she'd scold, mutter reprimands, and occasionally commit minor mischief, such as releasing someone's cattle.

Poverty, eccentricity, and mischievous antics caught up with Sarah when she was hauled into court and accused of witchcraft. Typically disrespectful, she responded to the magistrates in a spiteful and abusive manner.

Her own six-year-old daughter, Dorcas, was terrorized into testifying against her. Her timid husband, William, would not speak on her behalf. Although pregnant at the time of her arrest, she and Dorcas were locked away in the humiliating confines of Salem Jail. There Sarah's child was born and died.

Still, Salem's assistant minister, the pious and pitiless Nicholas Noyes, tried to coax a confession out of her. After all, he reasoned, "she *knew* she was a witch."

But to the last Sarah defended herself with outspoken precision. She responded to the self-righteous cleric with what might be described as "a holy curse."

"You are a liar," she said. "I am no more a witch than you are a wizard. And if you take away my life, God will give you blood to drink."

Sarah Good was hanged on July 19, 1692.

Apparently the Reverend Noyes didn't take her dying curse very seriously; perhaps he should have been more astute.

The merciless minister died of an internal hemorrhage, bleeding profusely from the mouth—drowned in his own blood.

## CAUSING EFFECTS

Sometimes the *effect* of a curse is obvious, but the *cause* is not apparent. In these cases someone identifies an unrelenting string of bad luck that seems to occur with no traceable reason. To the superstitious mind such a sinister succession of events *must* have been propelled by a curse, although there may well be no record of its having been uttered. Sometimes a curse story is retrofitted to suit the unfortunate chain of circumstances. Sometimes the cause for the ill luck remains a mystery. Perhaps the Hope Diamond fits this category. Crystals and gemstones are believed to be able to retain supernatural energy, almost like batteries. Louis XVI purchased the Hope Diamond in 1668. Since then all its owners have experienced sickness, ill luck, or untimely death.

A comparable example exists in twentieth-century Greenwich, Connecticut, at Dunnellen Hall, a twenty-eight-room mansion constructed in 1918 on twenty-six acres near Long Island Sound.

This Jacobean behemoth was built by Daniel Grey Reid as a wedding present for his daughter Rhea and her husband, Henry Ropping. Presumably the place wasn't born bad, but, somewhere along the way, something happened. Over the years it has picked up the reputation of bringing bad financial luck to everyone who's occupied it since the Roppings sold it in 1950 to steel magnate Loring Washburn. Almost immediately he was beset with money problems. Things got so bad that in the early 1960s the finance company took his house away.

The huge mansion remained vacant for years, and locals began calling it a haunted house. The ex-wife of an heir to the Dodge automobile fortune finally bought Dunnellen. A former showgirl, she married Daniel Moran, a New York City cop who later shot himself. She sold it in 1968 to Jack Dick, a financier, who paid $1 million for the place. Three years later he was indicted for stealing $840,000. Before the case went to trial in 1974, Jack died of a heart attack as he was being chauffeured home.

Lydia, his widow, promptly put the house up for sale. It was she who first gave voice to what many others suspected: The place was cursed. Like the Hope Diamond, it brought bad luck to everyone who owned it.

Nonetheless, Indian oilman Ravi Tikkoo readily laid down $3 million to buy the "cursed" property. He was quickly seized with unexpected financial problems associated with the mid-1970s oil embargo. Soon he was forced to sell.

At this point Harry and Leona Helmsley acquired Dunnellen Hall. Shortly thereafter the feds caught up with them. In 1988 the Helmsleys were arrested for income tax evasion, and in 1990 Leona—the so-called Queen of Mean—was convicted and sentenced to prison.

I can't help but wonder if the Ropping family somehow saw what was coming and unloaded the place just in time.

## LAST CHANCE TO TURN BACK

In the following pages we will witness a variety of New England curses at work, with all their attendant horror, pathos, and occasional humor.

Please keep in mind that this book is not intended to be all-inclusive. The sheer volume of Yankee maledictions would make that impossible.

At the very least, what you hold in your hands should be a collection of entertaining stories. At most, it is evidence that there are powers in this world so subtle and sinister that they can work inexorably against us without our even knowing it.

In the interest of journalistic objectivity, I haven't taken a position one way or the other. All I can tell you is that I have visited Black Agnes many times, and I have never chosen to sit on "her" lap.

# "A DREADFUL WIZARD"

*"Giles Corey," said the Magistrate,*
*"What hast thou heare to pleade*
*To these that now accuse thy soule*
*Of crimes and horrid deed?"*
*Giles Corey, he said not a worde,*
*No single worde spoke he.*
*"Giles Corey," saith the Magistrate,*
*"We'll press it out of thee."*

—Anonymous, from an old ballad

## OUTSIDE THE LAW

A battle was raging in 1692 Salem, Massachusetts. A battle of good versus evil. But as history demonstrates, the combatants were not only mismatched but also mislabeled.

In that most maniacal of times, the "Good People" of the Puritan village carted a pitiable parade of townspeople to the gallows. In all, nineteen men and women, and two dogs, met their ends dangling from ropes on Gallows Hill.

This is the story of an accused witch—"a dreadful wizard"—who escaped the noose but, though never tried or convicted, was executed anyway.

And it is the story of the revenge he exacted against certain of his tormenters.

The details of the Salem witch trials have been told by many writers, and speculation about what caused the murderous madness is well known to most readers. Theories range from teenage hysteria, to neighborhood grudges, to hallucinogenic foods, to over-the-top religious fever, to opportunistic land grabbers, to church rivalry, and include a motivational witch's brew that blends all the above and more.

## CRUEL AND UNUSUAL PUNISHMENT

Goodman Giles Corey was one of the more successful citizens of Salem. Years of hard work had produced a prosperous farm, and he had invested wisely. At eighty he was still a formidable fellow.

Martha was his third wife. His first wife, Margaret, had given him only daughters, but she had died after the birth of their fourth girl. Then, in 1664, Giles married Mary. Apparently they got along well and raised his daughters together.

Giles purchased a 150-acre farm, where he employed several farmhands. Despite all this, Giles's reputation was—at least in Puritan terms—less than sterling.

In his youth he had been a brute of a man, powerful, large, and authoritative. One day Jacob Goodell, a hired hand, was found badly beaten. Local scuttlebutt was that Giles had thrashed him because of his sloppy work habits. When Jacob died, townspeople took Giles Corey to trial. Their case was weak, and Giles was found innocent.

A second incident contributed to Giles Corey's blemished name. Another employee, John Gloyd, sued him for back wages. The case never went to court but was settled by arbitrators, who found in favor of the hired man.

One of these arbitrators was John Proctor. A few days later the Proctors' house caught fire. Again Giles was under suspicion, but a formal hearing found him innocent.

After Mary's death in 1684, Giles married his third wife, the kindly, "prayerful" Martha.

They lived well, as Giles's holdings were substantial. He was older now. The years and his good-tempered wife had a calming effect on him. He repented his sins, became more congenial and friendly, even joined Martha regularly at church services. When the Salem Witch Trials began in February of 1692, Giles and Martha Corey were some of the first people to attend the pre-trial examinations at the Salem Village Meetinghouse. As the examinations went on, Martha started to question the motives and claims of the accusers; she even tried to persuade her husband from attending further examinations by hiding his riding saddle. The townspeople began to believe that anyone who refused to decry witchcraft must be guilty themselves, and Martha Corey's actions made her seem suspicious. By mid-March, the witch-crazed girls cried out against Martha. Their accusations turned even her husband against her. Giles became swept up in the mass hysteria and testified against Martha on March 24. Giles spoke of sudden illnesses that afflicted household animals. He testified that his wife would appear to be praying by the fire late into the night, without uttering audible prayers, according to historian and author Rebecca Beatrice Brooks.

Perhaps Goodman Corey thought his testimony would protect him, but it wasn't long before his wife's accusers turned their vengeful lies against him. In April 1692 Ann Putnam Jr., Mercy Lewis, Abigail Williams, and others attested that Giles Corey was "a dreadful wizard."

On April 18 Giles was hauled in, examined by the magistrates, and thrown into prison where, languishing with his wife, they awaited trial.

Five months later, the eighty-year-old farmer, landowner, and full member of the church was brought before the Court of Oyer and Terminer. The court brought up Corey's previous testimony against his wife and tried to get him to provide more incriminating information, but this time Corey refused. In fact, he refused to say anything further, even to declare his innocence.

The next crucial question in the ritualized proceeding was to ask if he would be tried by God and his country (meaning a jury).

Giles Corey remained silent. His silence, in effect, meant that he refused to agree to be tried. He was therefore denying the court's right to try him.

This tactic left Judges Sewall, Hathorne, and Stoughton in a quandary: They couldn't proceed with a trial without his consent. And—strictly speaking—they couldn't convict him without a trial.

We'll never know for certain why Giles Corey refused to participate in his own defense. He probably realized that defending himself would do no good. All others who had denied the charges of witchcraft, regardless of the strength of their cases, had been found guilty and hanged anyway. And while those who said they were guilty of witchcraft were not hanged, they were instead condemned to jail and forced to forfeit all they possessed. For Giles Corey it was a lose–lose situation. Perhaps silence was the only way the elderly farmer could express his disapproval of the proceedings and his contempt for the accusing teenagers, the pompous magistrates, and the thieving sheriff.

But Giles was a clever man, and his motives were no doubt loftier than simple contempt. He must have realized that, under English law, if he didn't participate in the trial, he could leave his property to whomever he pleased. If he were tried and found guilty, however, he would forfeit all his possessions and vast land holdings. To speak would be to deny his heirs their rightful inheritance and to further line the pockets of the avaricious sheriff, who would confiscate everything, just as he had with others who had climbed Gallows Hill.

Whatever his motive, Giles Corey remained as silent as stone.

But English law permitted the judges to punish him for nonparticipation. In fact, English law even prescribed what that punishment might be: the atrocious *peine forte et dure*. Meaning "strong and hard punishment," it was a technique straight out of the Dark Ages. One catch: It was illegal in colonial Massachusetts, and for two very good reasons. First, there was no law that permitted it. And second, it violated the provisions of the "Body of Liberties" that, supposedly, ended barbarous punishments in the New World.

Nonetheless, the impatient Puritan judges decided to ignore their own law, which stated, "for bodily punishment we allow amongst us none that are inhumane, barbarous or cruel."

So they opted for a technique that could not possibly be any more inhumane, barbarous, or cruel. They turned the old man over to Judge Corwin's nephew, George Corwin, the high sheriff of Essex County, for a punishment that was, without doubt, the most heinous abomination ever carried out in the name of justice in the history of America.

Giles Corey was to be its first and last victim.

The morning of Monday, September 19, 1692, Sheriff Corwin and his henchmen stripped the old man and dragged him, in heavy chains, from the witch dungeon. Townspeople followed the procession, gawking and jeering.

They slowly proceeded to an open field not far from the jail, where a shallow rectangular pit had been dug in the earth. Using period maps, journal entries, and other first-hand accounts, modern historical researchers believe that the location of the pit was either the Pytharg lot across from the jail, or in the

yard of Thomas Putnam, whose daughter Ann had been one of the Coreys' accusers.

Giles Corey was forced to lie down upon a plank within this grave-like depression.

"Will you submit to be tried?" Sheriff Corwin demanded. Perhaps there was a twinkle in the lawman's eyes, for no matter how the old man responded, the sheriff would have something to gain. An affirmative answer would allow him to claim all Giles Corey's worldly goods. No answer would permit the sadistic sheriff to proceed with the torture.

Giles Corey squinted up at the New England sky and remained silent.

The deputies placed another heavy wooden plank over Goodman Corey's torso, then, one by one, heavy stones and bricks were piled on top of the plank. These pressed heavily on Giles's stomach and chest.

Still the old man did not cry out.

"Do you submit?" Sheriff Corwin repeated.

The only reply was the subtle sound of rocks scraping together as the old man tried to breathe.

Over time more and more rocks were added, and the question was repeated. But always Giles Corey remained silent.

The pressing lasted for two grueling days. During that time the prisoner was permitted only three mouthfuls of bread and three sips of water.

As stones were added, it became increasingly difficult for Giles to breathe. Eventually it would become impossible. If he were lucky, his rib cage would shatter under the weight, and death would come quickly. But apparently the old man had sturdy bones, and the torture continued.

From time to time Sheriff Corwin would mount the boulders and stare down at his helpless victim. "Are you prepared to be tried by God and Country?" he'd growl.

On one occasion the old man's lips moved. Eagerly, one of the sheriff's minions bent down to hear the faint reply.

"What does he say?" demanded Sheriff Corwin.

"More weight!" said the astonished deputy.

When the load had increased sufficiently, Giles Corey's face took on a livid red glow. His eyes began to bulge. With the addition of another two or three boulders, his tongue protruded from his mouth. Robert Calef, a witness, recorded that "the Sheriff with his Cane forced it in again."

Finally, with the unrelenting weight squeezing the last breath from his lungs, Giles Corey uttered his final words. "Damn you Sheriff," he said. "I curse you and I curse Salem."

Then—with nearly 200 good and pious Puritans looking on—Giles Corey was gone.

On September 22, two days after Giles's death, his wife Martha was among the last group of people to be hanged at Gallows Hill.

Goodman Corey and his wife both fell victim to that period of schizophrenia in Salem's shameful past.

But such monstrous events reverberate for a long time.

Even today, something of Giles Corey remains . . .

## COREY'S CURSE

Perhaps it is unfortunate that, when Giles Corey issued his dying curse, he didn't name Sheriff George Corwin specifically. Instead, he cursed "the sheriff," and, in the ensuing years, many men have been elected to the office of "Sheriff of Essex County and Master and Keeper of the Salem Jail."

Author and oddity collector Robert Ellis Cahill served as sheriff of Essex County in the 1970s. He told me that he, and perhaps everyone else to have held the office, had been affected by Giles Corey's curse. He wrote, "All the High Sheriffs of this county before me, including Corwin, either died in office from heart problems, or retired with an ailment of the blood."

Giles Corey's tormenter, George Corwin, no doubt the cruelest sheriff in Essex County history, died of a heart attack in office in 1696. He was in his early thirties. By the time of his death, Sheriff Corwin was so hated by Salem townspeople that his family didn't dare bury him in the cemetery. Instead they entombed him temporarily in the basement of his own home (today Salem's Joshua Ward House) so that his enemies couldn't find him and desecrate his remains.

About 300 years later, in 1978, Robert Cahill—while in office—suffered a rare blood disease, a heart attack, and a stroke. Doctors could not find the cause of his afflictions. He was forced to retire as sheriff of Essex County and as Master and Keeper of the Salem Jail. Today he is living in Florida.

Mr. Cahill notes that the sheriff before him also contracted a serious blood ailment while in office; it forced him to retire. He, in turn, had inherited the post from his father after the elder man died of a heart attack . . . while serving as sheriff.

The previous sheriff had suffered heart problems as well. "So have all the others, as far back as I could trace," he says. "And the two men who've followed me have had an awful lot of trouble."

It is frightening to think that the aftershock of a curse uttered so long ago can target specific individuals three centuries later.

~

## GILES'S GHOST

Let us not forget that Giles Corey cursed not only the sheriff, but the city of Salem as well.

Nathaniel Hawthorne, author and apologetic descendent of Judge Hathorne, wrote, "Tradition was long current in Salem that at stated periods, the ghost of Giles Corey, the wizard, appeared on the spot where he had suffered, as the precursor of some calamity that was impending over the community, which the apparition came to announce."

Or, in the context of Giles's dying words, I might delete "to announce" and substitute "to cause."

Nathaniel tried to escape association with his witch-hanging Puritan ancestor by changing the spelling of his last name from *Hathorne* to *Hawthorne.* Salem Village changed its name to Danvers and by so doing may have dodged some portion of the Corey Curse.

But Salem itself has, for the most part, prospered. In part, I suppose, by commercially capitalizing on its sordid past.

Still, there have been periodic setbacks that may—by a certain stretch of the imagination—be attributed to Giles Corey's curse.

And those setbacks were always preceded by sightings of Giles's ghost.

In his entertaining book *Haunted Happenings,* Robert Cahill writes that the ghost was seen by many people just before Salem's most memorable twentieth-century disaster, the Great Fire of 1914.

People reported spotting a forlorn and ghastly figure, bent and twisted and wringing his bony hands as he floated among the old gravestones of the Howard Street Burying-Ground, near the Old Salem Jail and the sheriff's residence.

Subsequently, and perhaps coincidentally, the Great Fire started near Gallows Hill, where Giles Corey's wife and eighteen other innocent people were hanged. Wind-whipped flames raged toward the sea, wiping out about one-third of the city.

Curse or coincidence?

Robert Cahill has his own opinion.

## AUTHOR'S NOTE

Perhaps Giles Corey's cruel, slow death helped to turn the tide in Salem. After it, there seemed to be a sobering, a perceptible change of attitude. The witch hysteria began to subside. Many people saw Giles Corey as a martyr whose very public and prolonged demise helped turn opinion against the witchcraft trials.

And in time this most horrific of historical tragedies passed slowly into memory.

But those men elected high sheriff of Essex County and as Master and Keeper of the Salem Jail would never forget Giles Corey's last words.

Robert Cahill believed that he may have been the last sheriff to suffer the full force of Giles's wrath. In the same way that Salem Village may have escaped the brunt of the curse by changing its name to Danvers, sheriffs following Mr. Cahill may have dodged supernatural blows when the sheriff's office was moved from Salem to a new facility in Middleton. Technically speaking, Robert Ellis Cahill was the last sheriff to serve in Salem—and thus possibly the last victim of Giles Corey's curse. Cahill passed away at his home in Florida on June 19, 2005 at the age of 70.

# THE BURTON AIL

*Blighted be the grass that springs!*
*Blighted be all living things!*

—Charles J. Fox, "Death of Chocorua"

## AN INHOSPITABLE LAND

Although they are called the White Mountains, New Hampshire's spectacular peaks conceal many dark stories. And one, although horrific, is so filled with pathos that even New England bard John Greenleaf Whittier deemed it too sad to recount in verse.

It unfolds in the Sandwich Mountain range, some 20 miles south of Crawford Notch.

In the mid-1600s a small band of sturdy settlers began to trickle into the bleak, but beautiful, Swift River Valley. There, at the northeast base of a nameless mountain in a township not yet mapped, they erected a scattering of crude cabins and began to work the land.

None but the bravest, most hardy laborers would undertake the difficulties of carving out a town in such a desolate and distant place—the primeval forest. The very heart of a New World wilderness.

Swarms of summer insects, merciless winters, year-round predators, and an uneasy relationship with the native inhabitants could quickly lead to despair and desertion. But iron constitutions and an unerring sense of destiny held these early families in place.

Still, discouragement was part of life. Just as these pioneers seemed to be stockpiling supplies and getting a little ahead, bears, foxes, wolves, and other wild creatures would raid their larders or steal their pigs and calves, causing no end of damage.

Yet the land offered promise, and the surrounding forests were rich in beavers and other game.

Perhaps a certain peace of mind was won after the Dover Raid of 1686, when most of the native Abenaki abandoned the region. By 1700, following continued defeats by white soldiers, many had made their way to Canada and the St. Francis settlement on the St. Lawrence River.

But one, a young Pequawket chieftain and renowned shaman named Chocorua (pronounced *Chuck-ORE-oo-wa*), decided he could not leave. This was his homeland; his people had lived here for countless generations. His ancestors had died and were buried here.

Chocorua was a widower, a taciturn, haughty warrior with sad, dark eyes. He and his ten-year-old son—the only family he had left—had known no other home.

Father and son made friends with many of the settlers of the village. Chocorua helped them learn the ways of the woodland and gave them counsel in times of illness, sharing his knowledge of medicinal herbs, roots, and wildlife.

Eventually he developed a special fondness for the family of Cornelius Campbell, a gregarious Scot who lived within the developing town that would soon be called Burton.

Cornelius was a giant of a man with an intellect to match. Though his voice and manner were often harsh, he was good-hearted and capable of great tenderness—a natural leader. His wife, Caroline, came from a noble and prominent English family.

Like others in this tiny enclave, Cornelius Campbell had shunned the more populated portions of New Hampshire. If his politics had been different, he might have become a statesman.

But the Scot was no friend to the Stuarts, and, with the restoration of Charles II, he'd left England for the seclusion of the colonial wilderness.

In fact, he found the Native Americans far more agreeable than the English. Chocorua and his son were frequent guests at the Campbell homestead.

Cornelius had a son of his own. The boys—Indian and Anglo—were about the same age. Like their fathers, the youngsters became friends. The whole Campbell clan delighted at the way the Abenaki's son inspected their modest surroundings. They found great joy in the pleasure he took from sampling the delicious but unfamiliar wares of Mrs. Campbell's kitchen.

But Chocorua had a dark, brooding side, and sometimes he would wander off alone to an unusual peak nearby, a rugged, distinctively shaped dome with a treeless crest that looked like a jumbled pile of greenish granite. The Campbells thought of it as Chocorua's Mountain.

Perhaps he went there to meditate or to commune with the spirits of his forefathers, for the mountain had long been known to his tribe as a sacred place.

Indian tradition held that one dark night, many years before, the mountain gave forth a mysterious pyramid of flame. Samuel Adams Drake, in his *Heart of the White Mountains*, describes it this way:

> A brilliant circle of light, twenty miles in extent, surrounded the flaming peak like a halo; while underneath an immense tongue of forked flame licked the sides of the summit with devouring haste. . . . In the morning a few charred trunks, standing erect, were all that remained of the original forest. The rocks themselves bear witness to the intense heat which has either cracked them wide open, crumbled them in pieces, or divested them, like oysters, of their outer shell, all along the path of the conflagration.

From no two viewpoints does the mountain appear the same. Depending on your position, it can resemble a breaking wave, a horn, a helmet, even a sleeping Indian with perfect features, feathers, and shoulders. Thus for the Indians, the mountain was infused with power, a magic place.

For Chocorua, his mysterious mountaintop sanctuary was a connection with the old ways. Sometimes, while on these mystical retreats, Chocorua would leave his son in the care of the Campbells.

The two boys always enjoyed their time together, each learning the games and ways of the other. So when Chocorua had to travel north to the St. Francis settlement in Canada, he did not hesitate to leave his son with his friends, promising to return in a fortnight.

## A CHANGE OF CLIMATE

Meanwhile the Campbell farm was being repeatedly troubled by less desirable visitors—a pesky family of foxes. The boys made a game of trying to capture them, but it was to no avail. Shooting, Cornelius quickly discovered, was a waste of powder and ball; the sly little animals were simply too quick. Traps did no good; the intruders eluded them easily. So he prepared a bottle of poison with which he planned to saturate a quantity of fox bait.

During some idle moments the Indian boy found the bottle and, thinking it might be one of Caroline Campbell's delicious concoctions, took a long swallow. Though at first it seemed as sweet and thick as maple syrup, moments later he was racked with intolerable pain. Clutching his abdomen, he stumbled gagging and retching to the cabin, where Cornelius and Caroline did their best to save him.

They sat with him all night, taking turns wiping his brow with cool water and whispering encouraging words and prayers. By morning the young man had faded into a calm sleep from which he drifted away to join his ancestors.

Cornelius and his son buried their young friend by a big stone at the edge of the forest.

When Chocorua returned he was inconsolable. Whatever trust he had formed for the white man evaporated instantly. He would not believe that his son's death was an accident, the consequence of the boy's ignorance. No! It was the white man's treachery. He never should have trusted Campbell. He never should have trusted anyone!

With the stealth of a catamount, Chocorua vanished into the forest.

"Give him time," Caroline Campbell told her husband. "He's an intelligent man. In God's time he'll come to understand."

Cornelius wasn't so sure. "I pray you are not mistaken."

### ANOTHER NIGHTMARE

Some days later Cornelius saddled his horse—the only means of conveyance, there being no wagons or wagon roads—with the intention of carrying a bushel of corn to the mill, 10 miles away.

When he returned home that evening, he stepped into a nightmare. He found his wife and son on the floor of their cabin, butchered beyond recognition.

There could be no doubt about who had committed the atrocity and why. Seized by a demonic compulsion for revenge,

Cornelius Campbell set out. He knew exactly where he had to go.

Tracking would be unnecessary. Still, a disturbance in the dust, a torn blade of grass, a severed leaf, all told the same story. Chocorua had gone to the mountain.

Cornelius followed the trail through bush, swamp, and woodland, then scrambled up the steep slopes to Chocorua's peak.

He found the Indian where he knew he would be. The young chieftain was seated on a table-size rectangle of rock at the mountaintop, 3,475 feet above the town of Burton.

From there the whole world could be seen, but the two men saw only each other. Now neither's wrath could be tempered by mercy. There was no possibility of discussion or compromise. All memory of their families' friendship had frozen into unrelenting hatred.

"Jump," commanded Cornelius, raising his flintlock and aiming it at Chocorua's chest.

The chief glared at his former friend. "The Great Spirit gave life to Chocorua," he said. "Chocorua will not throw it away at the command of a white man!"

The Scot pressed his rifle tight against his shoulder. "Then hear your 'Great Spirit' speak in the white man's thunder!"

Chocorua didn't move. He lifted his hands, not in supplication or surrender, but as if to summon the very forces of the sky and earth. Then, without removing his eyes from those of his enemy, he spoke:

"May the Great Spirit curse you. When he speaks in the clouds, his words are fire! Lightning blast your crops! Wind and fire destroy your homes! May the Evil One breathe death upon your cattle! Panthers and wolves will fatten on your bones! Chocorua goes to the Great Spirit—but his curse stays with the white man!"

Cornelius Campbell pulled the trigger. Powder flashed. The explosion of his gun rumbled like thunder through the White Mountains.

It is uncertain whether his musket ball struck the Indian, or whether Chocorua turned and plunged over the cliff to his death.

## THE NIGHTMARE CONTINUES

Later—after telling the tale to his neighbors—a distraught Cornelius Campbell recovered the mangled remains of his fallen friend and buried him near the Tamworth path.

But the balance of nature, and supernature, were not restored. For it is a fact that Chocorua's Curse came to pass.

Renewed Indian attacks were the first sign. Tomahawks and scalping knives, so long at rest, were busy again among the settlers. Terrible windstorms uprooted trees and hurled them at their dwellings. Settlers attributed renewed wolf and bear raids to this Indian curse.

Other things went terribly wrong—things that could not be accounted for. Crops withered and died. Sickness felled the strongest men.

Most troubling, perhaps, was the mysterious death of their cattle, a main source of sustenance. It became impossible to raise a calf. They were stillborn or would expire without taking their first step.

Under its inexplicable handicap, the village of Burton did not grow as fast as the neighboring towns. People began to refer to their trouble as the "Burton Ail," while quietly whispering of Chocorua's Curse.

It all became more terrifying when death extended its reach beyond Burton to nearby towns. As far away as Jackson, cattle lost weight and dropped in the fields.

All over the region crops, animals, and people began to waste away. Robust men became fragile, walking skeletons.

Pestilence and storm devastated much of the surrounding countryside. Burton, like many smaller settlements, was all but abandoned.

Oddly, Cornelius Campbell was untouched by the blight. While his crops and livestock suffered, he remained straight and tall, growing more and more morose as he watched the devastation around him. Shunned by his sickly peers, he took to the woods and became a hermit. Two years later his corpse was discovered in his hut.

Convinced that the disease from which Burton cattle suffered could not be imaginary, one Professor Dana of Dartmouth College was sent into the afflicted town to investigate. In 1821 he theorized that the Burton Ail was, in fact, poisoned water. Wells, springs, the very groundwater contained a weak solution of muriate of lime. *That* was causing the problem.

This came as no surprise to the afflicted citizens. After all, such was the nature of curses: Cornelius Campbell had allegedly poisoned Chocorua's son, so Chocorua's magic had poisoned the town. Somehow, his shamanic powers saturated into the mountain and summoned the lime into the water.

Professor Dana suggested a natural remedy that might help: A certain kind of meadow mud administered in large pills to the cattle seemed to counteract the disease.

But the town's reputation still suffered because of the Burton Ail. Many townspeople thought a change of name would be beneficial. Eventually they renamed their town Albany.

But even with the change—all stamped, sealed, and legal—the curse did not cease. Cattle kept dying. Packs of wolves came down from the mountains, killing livestock and driving away game.

At night the few remaining families listened to the distant howling of unidentified creatures. The dismal wailing seemed to come from one particular peak, the one now called Mount Chocorua. Gradually the volume increased until the wailing became a bloodcurdling chorus.

Demons? Indian spirits?

The final echo of a curse uttered so very long ago?

## AUTHOR'S NOTE

The Burton Ail is a matter of historical record. Cattle did not live long in the region. They lost their appetite, pined, and died. Settlers suffered as well.

And Chief Chocorua was apparently a real person. Thorough historical documentation is difficult because Albany, New Hampshire's, records were lost in a fire many years ago. But Georgia Drew Merrill's *History of Carroll County* tells of an elderly settler of Tamworth, Joseph Gilman, who lived in the early years of the nineteenth century. He recalled and wrote about his frequent conversations with an older pioneer who claimed to have been on intimate terms with the Indian chief.

In any event, there can be no doubt that Chocorua has won a kind of immortality, and not just because of his curse. Today a mountain, a trail, a lake, a river, and a village all bear his name.

# THE SAGA OF
# THE SACO RIVER

*Les mères défendent à leurs enfants d'approcher de la rivière maudite*
*de peur qu'ils ne soient comptés parmi les noyés.*
*(The mothers forbade their children from approaching the cursed*
*river for fear they would number among the drowned.)*
　　　　　　　　　　　　　　　　　　　—Normand Beaupré, *Lumineau*

## A MAGICAL RIVER

Just east of Albany, New Hampshire, in the town of Conway, the curse-polluted waters of the Swift River merge with the Saco.

And the Saco River, like a 134-mile-long serpent, undulates southward from its birthplace in tiny Saco Lake, high in the White Mountains. It plunges south through Harts Location and into Conway, where it veers sharply east and crosses into Maine at the ancient glacial lakebed called the Fryeburg plain. From there its fickle flow meanders north, east, and then southward toward the twin towns of Saco and Biddeford, where it finally meets the sea at Saco Bay.

The Saco River was once an Indian route from the White Mountains to the Atlantic; all the land through which it zigzags was Native land.

In 1609 Richard Vines, a British-educated physician, along with other pioneers, was sent to explore Maine and to found a settlement. This he did in 1616 at Winter Harbor, near the mouth of Saco River.

Subsequently, permanent settlers began to arrive. By 1631 both sides of the river were considered as one town, known first as Saco, and after 1718 as Biddeford.

In one capacity or another, Richard Vines governed there until 1645, when rival claims to the province irritated him so much that he resigned, packed up, and returned to England. Not long afterward, in 1647, the Massachusetts Bay Colony claimed jurisdiction. Between then and the time it became a state in 1820, Maine was considered part of Massachusetts.

But long before Richard Vines or any other white man arrived, the area was populated by Indians.

The dramatic falls (where today Main Street crosses the Saco River, between Saco and Biddeford) was a productive seasonal spot for hunting and fishing. Natives and newcomers enjoyed the bounty of the land and water.

In fact, during Richard Vines's tenure, newcomers seemed to enjoy an extraordinarily harmonious relationship with the indigenous people. This was in conspicuous contrast with the bloody Pequot War that savaged Massachusetts, Rhode Island, and Connecticut.

But this harmony cannot be solely attributed to Richard Vines and the other white men.

On Indian Island (today called Factory Island) there lived a young Indian chief named Squando. He was a friend and frequent visitor to his white neighbors. A dignified leader and articulate ambassador, Squando commanded the respect of all who knew him.

Although there is little written history about him, many stories passed down through the generations reveal his honorable nature. For example, settlers told how when Squando came across a young white captive who'd been abducted by Indians farther north in Maine, he personally took her from her captors and delivered her safely to the nearest white settlement.

Among his own people, the Sokokis tribe, Squando was not only the sagamore, or chief, but he was also regarded as a powerful magician.

All accounts—Indian and Anglo—agree that suddenly he was changed from friend to enemy by a needless and preposterous event that happened on the Saco River in the summer of 1675. And with it, local Indian sympathies changed, aligning more with those of the war-making Wampanoag leader, King Philip.

As with King Philip's War, it seems to be the English who started the trouble.

The first recording of the incident was published in Boston in 1677, just two years after it occurred. But that account—as you might expect—blames Squando for the tragedy.

It is not my intention to blame one side or the other, merely to report what little we know about the story and its mysterious aftermath.

## AWAGIMISKA

According to Normand Beaupré's account in his book *Lumineau*, Squando was an exceptionally handsome man—strong, fearless, and uncommonly wise. He was single and therefore much desired by the eligible young women of the tribe.

Despite all the attention from the fair sex, Squando took the responsibility of choosing a wife very seriously. She would, after all, give him the son who would inherit his authority as chief as well as the awesome power of his magical wisdom.

After much contemplation and spiritual introspection, he

picked a woman of rare character and beauty. Her name was Awagimiska.

Following a grand tribal ceremony with drums, dancing, gifts, and feasting, Squando and Awagimiska separated from the revelers and adjourned to his tepee. Everyone kept their distance after he let down the bearskin door.

## A SON IS BORN

Nine months later a baby boy was born. He came into the world precisely at the time the tribe's corn was sown, just as the first rays of the sun struck the summit of distant and mystical Mount Katahdin.

He was a beautiful boy with piercing eyes like a bald eagle. Squando named his son Mikoudou.

Before many months had passed, Awagimiska became aware that she would soon present Mikoudou with a brother or sister.

Squando was as proud as he was overjoyed. He went alone into the forest to thank the spirits that had provided for him so generously.

But a dark cloud was about to descend over the happy family, over Indian Island, and over the harmonious community that had so long lived there in peace.

## STRANGERS ARRIVE

An English ship had put in at the mouth of the Saco River, delivering a group of strangers into the seaside settlement.

Three seamen, perhaps after ingesting too much local rum,

decided to take a row upriver to see what was happening on Indian Island. It was a beautiful summer day.

They splashed along, smacking the water with their oars, shouting, singing, and drinking. Soon they noted with pleasure a lovely young Indian woman crossing the channel in a canoe. They had no way of knowing this was Awagimiska, wife of the local chief. With her, just out of sight in the bottom of the canoe, was their infant son, Mikoudou, wrapped in a blanket to protect his soft skin from the summer sun.

English attention shifted from the woman when she stopped paddling and picked up the squirming child.

"Look at that," one said, "the bitch has its whelp."

Then one of the three recalled an age-old debate about these New World "savages."

"It is said," the first seaman declared to his mates, "that these Indian brats can swim from the day they are born. They do it naturally, never needing to be taught."

"Aye," the second said with a chuckle, "just like any animal, be it duck, dog, or beaver. They strike their paws beneath their throat like the dog, not spreading their arms as we do. I've heard it is so."

The third sailor lifted his eyebrows as if an idea had come to him. "What say you, then?" he said. "Shall we put it to the test?"

The three maneuvered their rowboat into the path of Awagimiska's canoe. One cradled his rum bottle as if it were an infant, grinning toothlessly. "That papoose of yours," he asked, "does it swim with the skill of an otter?"

But the frightened woman could not understand his words, nor the reason for his mocking tone.

"Let us see, then," said the man, reaching out for the baby.

Awagimiska tried to paddle away, but an Englishman had seized her canoe and pulled it alongside. She fought to keep her son from the clutches of the groping strangers. Hands like fat white spiders filled the air. The canoe tipped and lurched, and suddenly rough fingers clutched her.

She begged them to leave her son alone, but they didn't understand or didn't care. Now the nearest white man was pulling Mikoudou from her grasp.

She heard a splash.

A tiny bundle, wrapped in a blanket, bobbed briefly and sank in the river's current.

With a cry of pain and a great seizure of strength, Awagimiska pulled away from her jeering captors. Rolling over the side of the canoe, she took a breath and plunged into the cold water, searching for her son. She reached out to grab him, but her fingers clutched only the blanket. She cast it aside, her head snapping this way and that, hoping for a glimpse of her baby.

She knew she could not return to the surface without Mikoudou.

"'Tis my belief the argument is settled, then," said one of the three Englishmen.

"Aye, the little savages cannot swim. Nor can their mothers."

As the two men laughed, the third sailor stared at the undisturbed surface of the water as the empty birchbark canoe drifted silently away.

## SQUANDO'S REVENGE

When he heard the news that his wife, son, and unborn child had drowned, Squando was provoked beyond reason or recon-

ciliation. Soon, as chief, he would lead his people to join King Philip's War.

But now, as sorcerer, he waded into the waters of the Saco River. There, knee-deep, he raised his arms and called upon the spirits of the river to assist in his revenge.

Squando laid a curse upon the river, requiring that each year its waters would claim the lives of three white men: one drowning for each of his three lost family members, one death for each of their three assassins.

And so it was for years and years to come. The Saco River became a cursed river, a river of death.

## AUTHOR'S NOTE

As recently as 1931, the *Portland (Maine) Sunday Telegraph* reported, "It is a curious fact that since that year when the curse was pronounced [1675] three white people each year have died by drowning in the Saco River!"

To what degree the curse survives to this day is a matter of conjecture. No one is indelicate enough to keep a toll of annual hits and misses.

In 1947 the same newspaper reported, "Saco River Outlives Curse," suggesting that for the first time the full quota had not been met.

In 2001 at least two people died on the Saco River—a man drowned in Fryeburg, and a swimmer jumped from a bridge and broke his neck. In 2002 the river claimed the life of an eleven-year-old boy. He vanished while swimming with some friends. The next day police found his body 75 feet downriver in 10 feet of water.

And the legend continues, weakened perhaps, but alive in the minds of the people in the Saco-Biddeford area. Each summer they speak of the three yearly drownings, and watch to see if the curse holds true.

Even now it is said that some parents will not let their children approach the river until news of the third drowning is made public.

# A Blighted Campaign

*One other post…still remained in the hands of the enemy. This was the village of St. Francis, situated at the mouth of the river of that name between Montreal and Quebec. From its easy communication with the upper part of the Connecticut River, this place had long been a focus of murder and devastation and many a captive had there suffered barbarities intolerable; and the place was loaded with the plunder of the English colonies. General Amherst now resolved to put an end to these barbarities by destroying the place.*

–Rev. Henry H. Saunderson, *History of Charlestown, New Hampshire*

## ORDERS

Y ou are this night to . . . proceed to Misisquoy Bay, from whence you will march and attack the enemy's settlements on the south-side of the St. Lawrence, in such a manner as you shall judge most effectual to disgrace the enemy, and for the success and honor of his Majesty's arms."

This, in part, was the order issued by Lord Jeffrey Amherst to Maj. Robert Rogers, instructing him to attack the St. Francis Indians.

The next day, September 12, 1759, Major Rogers set out from the fort at Crown Point with a body of 200 men, heading north by boat on Lake Champlain. Their destination—and target—was Odanak, the largest known Abenaki settlement in the region, known as the village of St. Francis.

Situated at the mouth of the St. Francis River where it meets the St. Lawrence, the village was about halfway between Montreal and Quebec City. The whole trip would plunge green-clad Rangers and green recruits hundreds of miles into enemy territory, first by water, then over land.

The planned raid was chiefly retaliatory, but the English also believed a devastating strike would discourage Indians from supporting the French during a forthcoming raid on Montreal.

That raid, planned for the spring of 1760, would never happen. And this one—perhaps from the start—was doomed to be a blighted campaign for English and Indian alike.

Misfortunes began on the twentieth of the month, as the Rangers entered the northern reaches of Lake Champlain. A keg of gunpowder mysteriously exploded. Forty disabled Rangers were sent back to Crown Point, leaving Major Rogers with 160 men.

At Missisquoi Bay they beached their boats, concealing them along with provisions for the return trip. But as Major Rogers soon learned, Abenaki guards from a deserted Indian village nearby had discovered the boats and supplies and removed everything.

This meant the Rangers would have to find an alternate, safer return route. It also meant the newly alerted French and Indians would soon be at their back. Rogers's Rangers would either have to stand and fight or press on, outmarching their pursuers.

Major Rogers chose the latter. It was the only way he could accomplish his objective.

He sent Lieutenant McMillen, along with ten men, back to Crown Point to tell General Amherst they'd been discovered. He also requested that provisions be sent from Fort Number 4 at Charlestown, New Hampshire, up the Connecticut River, which would become the Rangers' new return route.

There were now 149 men. Major Rogers had already lost one quarter of his forces—and the battle hadn't even begun.

Now more than ever, speed became essential. Major Rogers pushed his men through the wet, inhospitable wilderness. Some areas were covered with thigh-deep water. In order to rest, the men had to fabricate crude hammocks from spruce boughs. But they could pause only briefly, for they knew the French and Indians couldn't be far behind.

Day after day they marched from early dawn till darkness. During this cruel passage some took sick and some deserted. Their number shrank by another eighteen. Major Rogers was reduced to 131 men before laying eyes on Odanak.

As the men pushed north, a scout named Deluth had a curious encounter. It seemed to be with some variety of wild man: neither French nor Indian, neither human nor animal. Deluth described it as looking like "a large black bear, who would throw large pine cones and nuts down upon us from the trees and ledges."

An oddly intelligent bear?

Perhaps. But—considering all the strange things that were to follow—it may have been an omen, something of a supernatural caution sign, warning the men to proceed no farther, warning them of the horrors that lay ahead.

## DEEPER INTO DARKNESS

Under the relentless command of Robert Rogers, the Rangers and the enlisted men continued their struggle northward. The Rangers were used to hardship. That's why Lord Jeffrey had sent them. Major Rogers's men could do what the traditional English redcoats could not. An elite fighting team, they were as adept with flintlocks as tomahawks, and trained to fight like Indian guerrillas, striking silently, invisibly, swiftly, then vanishing like ghosts.

On the tenth day after leaving Missisquoi Bay, the men arrived at the St. Francis River, about 15 miles above the targeted Indian village of Odanak. After fording the rapidly flowing water, they at last found themselves on firm marching ground.

Now, twenty-two days after leaving Crown Point, Major Rogers climbed a tree and—for the first time—saw his target village some 3 miles away.

## ODANAK

Here they stopped and refreshed themselves. But knowing that the French with their Indian allies might be gaining on them, they dared not rest for long. At eight o'clock that evening Major Rogers, Lieutenant Turner, and Ensign Avery disguised themselves as Indians and left the company to reconnoiter the settlement.

Odanak, the St. Francis Indian village, had been a center of French and Indian interaction for nearly a century. The French had established a mission there to convert the local Indians. Most residents—a ragtag population from decimated tribes like Anasagunticooks, Ameriscoggins, Pequawkets, Cooashaukes, and other members of the Abenaki Nation—had converted to Catholicism.

Major Rogers observed that an 8-foot wooden stockade surrounded about fifty wigwams made from poles covered with bark and skins.

At the very center stood the Catholic church.

He reported that the Indians were engaged in "high frolick" (actually they were celebrating a chief's wedding) and were clearly oblivious to the enemy lurking so near.

*This*, the major thought, *is a bit of good luck. The savages will retire late. They'll be nearly as exhausted as we are.*

At three o'clock in the morning, Major Rogers advanced with his whole party. Within 300 yards of the village, the men prepared for action.

When first light came—as Major Rogers later wrote in his letter to General Amherst—they "discovered and destroyed the town."

This may be one of the grandest understatements in colonial American history. In reality, the devastating action unfolded something like this:

One hundred thirty-one Rangers attacked from three points, easily assailing the stockade walls. The Indians had no warning until the invaders burst into their homes, slaughtering them in their beds.

Some—dazed and bewildered—staggered into the streets only to be cut down by musket balls and bayonets.

The stench of gunpowder mingled with cries of terror in the morning air.

A few Indians dove into the river, but this escape route had been anticipated. Sharpshooters picked them off like floundering ducks. Those who made it to their canoes were also in for a surprise. The Rangers had punctured the vessels just above the waterline. The added weight of the fleeing Indians sank the boats. Any who did not drown fell to musket balls.

The butchery continued for two full hours. At first, in the indistinct light of dawn amid the haze of musket smoke, it was difficult for the Rangers to differentiate the young and old, the elderly and infirm, the boys and girls—so they cut down everyone without prejudice. As daylight brightened, their fury was exacerbated by the sight of 600 English scalps drying in the breeze. With that, any possibility of restraint was lost. Knives, guns, and tomahawks did their terrible business. The Rangers took some scalps of their own.

## NO SANCTUARY

Due to its ghastly nature, the next part of the story is rarely told. Even Kenneth Roberts deleted the atrocity from his comprehensive historical novel *Northwest Passage.*

A small group of terrified Abenakis scrambled for the church with the bloodthirsty Rangers in pursuit. Inside the chapel candles were burning, lending a false sensation of tranquility. But there was to be no sanctuary.

Father Virot, the Jesuit priest, interposed himself between the savage Englishmen and the cowering Indians. For a moment all was still as the Rangers gawked, surprised at the treasures within the humble church: golden candlesticks, silver plates, bejeweled chalices. But the gem that arrested all eyes was a solid silver statue of the Madonna.

Finally Ranger Benjamin Bradley stepped forward, eye to eye with the priest.

"Madmen," Father Virot said, "for the sake of Him on the Cross, stay your hands! This is the house of God!"

Benjamin Bradley hesitated only briefly. Outside, cries and gunshots filled the night. The thud of tomahawks beat an irregular rhythm as the Ranger raised his musket. "Yield, papist, and you shall have good quarter."

The Jesuit priest took the host from a golden chalice on the altar. With both hands he lifted the sacred wafer above his head as if it were a shield. Then, in a voice those who heard it would long remember, he commanded, "To your knees, monsters, to your knees!"

Ranger Bradley sneered and pulled the trigger. The holy man fell among the cowering Abenakis. A volley of rifle fire followed, slaughtering the Indians, filling the tiny church with blood.

∾

## VOICES OF THE DEAD

The whole confrontation took a mere ten minutes, leaving an eerie silence in the chapel. Slowly reanimating, some of the colonials ran from the slaughter. Others remained and began to plunder. They cleared the altar, stole the silver Virgin, and dashed the host to the ground.

But something was wrong.

A ghastly voice began to manifest from somewhere within the church. Somehow, it seemed to form from the reverberation of the priest's final words and the screams of the fallen Indians.

The looters froze, not sure what they were hearing, not sure where it was coming from. Perhaps it spoke from within the pile of corpses, perhaps from the very air. The exact words, articulated in English, were not recorded at the time. But—judging from those who recalled them later—there can be no doubt that a curse was placed upon the invaders. For the disembodied voice spoke as follows: "The Great Spirit will scatter darkness in your path. Hunger will walk before you and Death will strike your tail. Your wives will weep for the dead who will not return."

And then as a final chilling declaration, "Manitou is angry when the dead speak. The dead have spoken!"

For a heartbeat the Rangers were silent, stealing furtive glances at one another. Then, unwilling to betray fear to their comrades, they continued with their business.

"Manitou," one said. "What have we to fear from their Indian god?"

"Or the papist god, as well," answered another.

In a barrage of forced laughter, they checked to be sure they had all the valuables they could carry.

Then they torched the chapel and set fire to the rest of the village.

But flames would not deter the supernatural conflagration they had already ignited. As the Rangers began to depart, the bell in the burning chapel started to ring. Immobile with dread, they listened to the slow, measured tolling until the flaming belfry collapsed. The bell clanged to the ground, forever silent.

It was seven o'clock in the morning. The deed was done. The men were shaken, exhausted, but there was no time for rest.

Suspecting the French and Indians might be gaining rapidly, Major Rogers rushed his men away from the wasted settlement, commencing a trek that would be far worse than anything that had yet transpired.

## A DARK DESCENT

As a group they pushed in a southeasterly direction. Too tired to move quickly, but not daring to stop, they struggled onward. After their adrenaline surges had abated, the men realized how hungry they were. But shooting game or cooking a meal would only alert their pursuers.

Slowly, steadily, the remaining Rangers made their way as far as Little Forks—today's Lennoxville, Quebec, near Lake Memphremagog. Here they found the unfamiliar topography odd and unsettling, like something out of a nightmare. Kenneth Roberts describes it well in *Northwest Passage*:

Its hills and mountains are packed together like fish-balls on a platter; and wind, blowing between two hills and striking another, is twisted about so that it blows in circles. Thus rain-storms, instead of hitting trees properly and causing moss to grow on the northerly side, strike from all directions at once. As for the water-courses, there are brooks within half a mile of each other, flowing in four directions at the same time. Streams turn at right angles for no apparent reason, or make almost complete loops; and the valleys through which some of them flow are so deep and so involved that they seem to have been planned and dug by an insane god.

At this juncture the major decided it would be best to split up. He divided his 131 men and eight liberated captives into several parties; smaller groups, he explained, would be less visible, could move faster, and would find it easier to acquire game.

He ordered everyone to rendezvous on the Connecticut River where it meets the Passumpsic River, near present-day East Barnet, Vermont.

## DISAPPOINTMENT AND DESPAIR

And so the forced march continued, but things only got worse. Men dropped from exhaustion or bolted into the wilderness propelled by madness or fear.

Two days after separating, Ensign Avery's party was overtaken by the Indians. Seven men were captured; two escaped.

Another group of about twenty, under Lieutenants Dunbar and Turner, was attacked. Most were killed or taken prisoner, including the two officers.

The band under Major Rogers, after an exhausting march,

reached the point of rendezvous on the Connecticut River in a fearful state of starvation. The expected provisions were not waiting. No one was there to assist them.

A few of the men—near death already—were so disappointed that they expired before the next day.

## BRADLEY'S BAND

But it is Ranger Benjamin Bradley's group we want to follow.

Bradley, the priest killer.

Accompanied by eight other Rangers and bearing the pilfered wealth, they made their way south. An unseasonable snowstorm with freezing temperatures made progress difficult. Where, they wondered, had it come from? It seemed... unnatural.

Fear of pursuing Indians kept them from stopping long enough to seek nourishment. A crippling hunger quickly set in—just as the ominous voice had predicted. They often considered relieving themselves of the heavy silver burden, but even in their desperate state, such wealth was difficult to part with.

Eventually candlesticks, coins, and plates were jettisoned to lighten the load, but the silver statue was passed from hand to hand as one after another of the men fell away from exhaustion and died.

Half crazed with hunger and fatigue, only four emaciated Rangers finally made it to the Connecticut River. But they arrived at the wrong spot. Detecting no sign of other survivors, the men assumed they were the only ones to return alive from the raid. Frightened and disheartened, they crossed the river and continued pushing forth into the unrelenting wilderness.

Benjamin Bradley began to fantasize about continuing their hike all the way through the White Mountains and back to his home in Rumford, now Concord, New Hampshire.

It was then that the men experienced another curious encounter. As if in response to the major's reverie, an Indian appeared at their camp and offered to lead them through the "Great Pass" (Crawford Notch). Today, peering back through the hazy glass of history, it is difficult to tell whether this unexpected arrival was friend, enemy, apparition, or some malevolent minion of the malediction.

Before setting out with their new guide, they apparently hid some of the treasure at the mouth of Cow Brook (in today's North Littleton), then continued toward the darkness of the pass. The white hills, towering pines, and undisturbed snow presented a gloomy labyrinth.

In the great, dark distance an eerie howling—perhaps wolf or catamount—permitted them no peace. Their nerves continued to shatter like fragile ice.

When they were thoroughly buried in the impenetrable forest, their guide suddenly became fearful that the Great Spirit would kill him if he ventured farther. After making a crude—and apparently inaccurate—map for the starving Rangers, the Indian vanished into the wilds.

"We *are* cursed," Sergeant Parsons said over and over again. He had decided they were carrying their fate along with them in the form of the silver statue. More than once he recommended they dispose of it. The others would not listen.

But perhaps he was right. It wasn't much longer before the first of their tiny band went mad with hunger and fear. He threw himself over a cliff and fell to his death on the rocks below.

Somehow, the three survivors found the energy to bury their comrade—along with the rest of the treasure—in a cave. They planned to return for it later.

Then they staggered on for days without sustenance, racked with despair. Darkness filled the mountain paths; hunger lent torture to their every movement. They plodded, crept, and finally crawled on their bellies until madness possessed them.

Perhaps each died with the words of the curse echoing in his ears. For indeed, darkness had scattered their path, hunger had walked before them, and Death had inexorably struck them down in the frozen isolation of impenetrable mountains.

The next summer a hunter found Benjamin Bradley's skeleton; it was identified by the distinctive rawhide ribbon he wore.

Only one of the three, Sergeant Parsons, made it back to tell the tale. Gaunt, crazed, and strangely furtive, he carried six knives and a bloody knapsack containing the remains of the human head that had staved off his starvation.

## RELICS

Over the years many early settlers uncovered bones of Rogers's Rangers scattered amid the woods, rocks, and intervales.

And once in a while, bits of the St. Francis treasure have been recovered. In 1816 the golden candlesticks were dug up by a farmer pulling stumps near Lake Memphremagog. Volney Blodgett's gigantic barn in Waterford, Vermont, was financed with a cache of gold coins he found on his property.

As recently as May 1998, a woman from Potton, Quebec, found silver-coated plates in an eroding riverbank on her property. Called to investigate, historian Gérard Leduc determined that the plates had been in a fire and speculated they might have come from the Odanak raid.

The silver Madonna still awaits discovery somewhere along that fatal trek. Carefully hidden, or blasphemously hurled away, it will eventually be found by some treasure hunter or unwary hiker.

But whoever finds it should think twice before picking it up, because Sergeant Parsons may well have been right. Perhaps the curse of St. Francis lives on in that ten pounds of silver.

## AUTHOR'S NOTE

The French and Indian version of the St. Francis raid is, as you might expect, very different from that told by Major Rogers and General Amherst. The latter, fixed forever in the American memory by Kenneth Roberts's adventure novel *Northwest Passage*, gives an alternate picture. According to the French, only 30—not 200—Indians were killed.

Odanak was prepared for, not surprised by, the invasion. And there the discrepancies only begin. But of course, that is a different story . . .

# THE PHANTOM FOOT

*Two hundred Winters have not washed*
*The [B]ucksport stain away,*
*The foot is on the colonel's grave*
*Till the Judgement Day.*

–Robert P. Tristram Coffin

## A TOWN IN THE WILDERNESS

A deathbed curse has always been an especially fear-inducing form of malevolence. Uttered when someone is too weak for self-defense or retribution, it is a powerful wish. And if the doomed person's last wish is for revenge, the target of that vengeance had better beware. Though the avenger may be unable to strike out from this world, he or she is not far from the next. And who knows what manner of terror can be called down from the Other Side?

Perhaps New England's best-known example of a deathbed curse took place in Bucksport, Maine. The evidence is still there for all to see, right in the center of town. It's in the village cemetery, across from Hannaford's Supermarket and not far from the traffic light.

It's hard to believe black magic could be at work in such a mundane environment. But go. Take a look. Decide for yourself.

Here's the story—or at least one of them . . .

Col. Jonathan Buck founded the town of Bucksport in 1762, while Maine was still part of Massachusetts (and the United

States was still part of England). Rufus, the colonel's grandson, remembered him as "spare, thin . . . with an expressive face, Roman nose, black arching eyebrows, and dark, penetrating eyes."

He was known to be a man of iron will who built the town's first sawmill, the first gristmill, and even the first boat. He was considered an honorable, industrious gentleman, one well suited to life in what was then a near wilderness.

Colonel Buck served as local justice of the peace, responsible for administering the law throughout this seaside region. There was no question that the king's law was the colonel's law, and he was known to dispense English justice with an even, though iron, hand.

In many cases his judgments could be strict, Puritan-inspired, and—as was so often the case with Puritan justice—too rarely tempered with Christian forgiveness.

In one instance a woman named Ida Black was brought before him (in certain more romantic accounts, she's known as Ann Harraway). The specifics of Mistress Black's alleged crime have been lost to history. It must have been a capital offense, probably murder, but some local legends maintain she was tried for witchcraft.

In any event, she was found guilty and sentenced to be hanged. (Some accounts say she was burned at the stake, but as far as I know, no witches were ever burned in this country—not even in Maine.)

With the encouragement of the eager townspeople, Ida Black was marched to the gallows. But before the noose could do its work, she looked directly at Colonel Buck and spoke the last words her tongue would ever utter, something to the effect that, "You know I am innocent, so *you* are the guilty one. I will come back. And when I do, Jonathan Buck, I will dance on your grave!"

## GRAVEYARD DANCE

Her strange final words were soon forgotten, and Colonel Buck went on about the business of running his sawmill, grinding his grist, building his boats, and dispensing the king's justice. Everything went swimmingly in Bucksport until March 18, 1795, when the colonel himself passed away at age seventy-seven.

He was buried in the cemetery at the center of town.

Some years later, in 1852, a grand commomorative monument was erected in his honor—a giant obelisk of Blue Hill granite befitting such an important man. An inscription was carved upon it that read:

COL. JONATHAN BUCK

THE FOUNDER OF BUCKSPORT

AD 1762

BORN IN HAVERHILL MASS. 1718

DIED MARCH 18, 1795

For a while everything seemed to be fine. Then someone walking past the graveyard noticed that a peculiar shadow had fallen directly under the name BUCK.

Oddly, that strange shadow was visible on overcast days, and even at night.

Closer examination proved it wasn't really a shadow, but rather a mark on the stone itself. In the months that followed, the blemish expanded and darkened until anyone who saw it could easily recognize what it was: the outline of a leg, a leg about 24 inches long, complete with a foot attached, its toe pointed downward.

What was happening?

At first they thought it was the work of vandals. Then someone remembered the curse. Could the spirit of Ida Black have somehow returned to dance on the colonel's grave?

Suspecting pranksters, Colonel Buck's family hired a team of workmen to pumice down the monument, making it as smooth and unblemished as before. But the outline gradually reappeared. They tried more aggressive cleaning techniques, including sandblasting, chemical stain removers, and ultimately gouging out the stone's surface, but always the mysterious foot would return.

Finally—according to some of the locals—the family had the monument replaced. But when the hanged woman's dance continued on the new stone, the family gave up.

And there the monument stands to this day.

The mundane inscription, plus the mysterious foot, add up to a remarkable puzzle.

## AUTHOR'S NOTE

I suspect there is no better explanation than that of a curse.

We may fairly assume that the monument was perfect when it was erected. If it had been riddled with imperfections, the family would have sent the stonecutter back to the quarry for a new stone. Such imperfections—called inclusions—are obvious from the moment a stone is cut. They do not just appear like moisture bleeding through a basement floor. And if the mark were applied to the stone's surface later, after the monument was in place, professional cleaning techniques would have been successful.

As to the curse itself, Jennifer Marvin, who is married to one of Colonel Buck's descendants, says the Buck family tells a slightly different story. In a communication to the Roadside

America discussion board, she explains the variation, and adds a fascinating component to the tale.

Colonel Buck, she says, developed some sort of infatuation for a young Indian woman, who subsequently became pregnant. Since abortion was strictly prohibited in Puritan society, he did the next best thing: He burned the mother and unborn child. Some accounts say a detached leg rolled from the funeral pyre, as if reaching out to kick the adulterous colonel.

The young woman's mother, it seems, was a spiritual leader, or shaman, who may well have been locally described as a witch. In any event, she cursed Colonel Buck and his family, saying they'd never be rid of the murdered girl.

So in addition to the foot on the gravestone, every second generation produces a child with pronounced Native American features. Jennifer Marvin writes, "My mother-in-law and one of her sisters seem to have been the 'victims' of this curse—they both look of native heritage. Not one child born in my husband's generation has any trace of native features. We're all . . . curious to see . . . whose child will stand out from the rest of the family."

An interesting variation to be sure, but in the final analysis, I can't find any legitimate historical evidence that Colonel Buck was anything but an upstanding citizen and proper town father, deserving of having the town bear his name. So the "witch's curse"—if that's what it is—has stained more than his tombstone; it has stained his reputation as well. Now, in the twenty-first century, he is remembered only for an act of evil he probably never committed.

Today it is for us to consider who was wrongfully accused. And by whom.

As we stand before the colonel's tomb to contemplate the right and wrong of all this, perhaps we should take into consideration the outline of a heart that has appeared just as mysteriously on the upper spire of the monument.

It might well mean the colonel is now forgiven.

# THE MISSING MAN

*[H]is visage was remarkably wind-flushed, sun-burnt, and weather-worn, and had a most unquiet, nervous, and apprehensive expression. It seemed as if this man had some all-important object in view, some point of deepest interest to be decided, some momentous question to ask, might he but hope for a reply.*

–Nathaniel Hawthorne, "A Virtuoso's Collection"

## THE VOYAGE BEGINS

On a short trip from Concord, Massachusetts, to his home on Middle Street in Boston, Peter Rugg vanished forever.

Along with him his daughter Jenny, his horse Lightfoot, and his carriage all simultaneously blinked out of existence.

But strange to say, they're not gone all the time. Like the mysterious Flying Dutchman at sea, or the landlocked Wandering Jew, Peter Rugg puts in occasional, unpredictable appearances that leave witnesses with a peculiar sense of sympathy edged with terror. The last sighting, so I'm told, was in the 1940s, but it may be that he's out there yet, wandering the dirt roads of rural Rhode Island, or central Connecticut, or even the northern vicinity of Lake Champlain.

He's been spotted in all those places. And if he speaks, he asks the same question that he has asked for more than two centuries: "Can you show me the road to Boston?"

The strange story of Peter Rugg began in 1770, shortly before the American Revolution. He was a prosperous cattle and horse merchant with a growing business and a comfortable home on a corner lot in what we now call Boston's North End.

One fine fall morning he set off to Concord on a business trip. He hitched up his horse, a large Roman-nosed bay called Lightfoot. His wagon was small and easy for the powerful animal to pull. When Peter was about to depart, his daughter Jenny approached him with a request: "Father, may I ride along with you?"

"Indeed you may, my child. But make haste, for our trip is one of business, not pleasure. And in arenas of commerce, it will never do to be unpunctual."

Jenny climbed aboard the wagon, proudly sitting next to her father as they clattered off down the cobblestone street.

Neighbors watched as the little girl looked around excitedly. She turned back to see her mother waving good-bye. There was no way for the child to know this was the last time their eyes would ever meet.

## TOM CUTTER'S TAVERN

The negotiations at Concord were concluded more slowly than Peter Rugg had planned. After expressing his disapproval—for Peter Rugg was known for his impatience and occasional outbursts of temper—father and daughter set off for their 25-mile return trip to Boston. Peter grumbled that if they had started back earlier, they might have escaped the rainstorm that was beginning to pelt the hard-packed earthen roadway.

Jenny snuggled closer to her father. He wrapped both of them in his cloak as the rhythm of the rain increased. Soon he could feel her shivering against his side. As they clattered into Menotomy (now West Cambridge), the sign for Tom Cutter's Tavern was a welcome sight.

Peter Rugg left his horse and wagon in the rain as he and Jenny slipped inside for a warm drink—a hot buttered rum for him, some warm milk for the little girl.

As Tom and Peter talked, the storm's fury increased. Thunder crashed violently as lightning ripped jagged patterns in the sky. Rain sounded like a river coursing across Tom Cutter's roof. The little girl stared frightfully at the window.

"Let me stable your horse, Peter. You and Jenny would do well to stay here the night," the innkeeper offered. "This tempest can't get anything but worse."

Peter swallowed the last of his rum and slammed his tankard down on the plank tabletop. "No sir. I told Mistress Rugg we'd be home tonight, and that is where we'll be. Come, Jenny."

Jenny stood up and hesitantly followed her father to the tavern door. Rain cascaded from the eaves like a waterfall; they could hardly see Lightfoot standing forlornly a short distance away.

"Don't be a fool, man," Tom Cutter protested. "It's a devil of a night and you both will catch a chill. Stay."

Without responding, and perhaps bristling at the word *fool*, the stubborn Dutchman picked up his daughter and splashed across the muddy yard to his wagon. He swung the girl into place, jumped in beside her, and was about to shake the reins when he discovered the soaking innkeeper at his side.

He grabbed Peter's arm. "Don't be a fool, Rugg," Tom said once more. "Night will soon be upon us, and this damned rain could be the death of your daughter. Can you not see that the storm is increasing in violence? For the Lord's sake, stay!"

With a rough tug, Peter jerked his arm from the innkeeper's grip. Temper flaring, he roared to the sky, "Let the storm increase. I will see home tonight in spite of storm or the Devil. Or may I never see home!"

With that he cracked his whip. The horse slogged forward.

Tom Cutter watched Peter Rugg, Jenny, Lightfoot, and the carriage disappear into the night.

## AMONG THE MISSING

Back home, Peter's wife reasoned that her husband had put up somewhere to wait out the storm. But when he and Jenny did not return the following day—or the next—she went to the authorities.

At first they took little action. But when a week had passed—reinforced by Mistress Rugg's continual goading—they launched a search.

Soon they realized the magnitude of the mystery on their hands. Somewhere in the short distance between Tom Cutter's Tavern in Menotomy and Middle Street in Boston, Peter Rugg, Jenny, their horse, and the carriage had vanished without a trace.

No one had seen or heard them after they departed the tavern.

Peter's wife spent a lonely winter in a drafty house that was far too big for her alone. By the time spring arrived, her reserves of hope had dwindled.

"If they are dead," she told her minister, "I could take comfort that they are with God. But not to know their fate. . . . Why, in that there is no comfort at all."

~

## A TROUBLED PAIR

The vanishing of Peter Rugg and Jenny remained a mystery and, for a while, was much talked about in Boston, Menotomy, and Concord. In time, however, everyone's mind—except of course that of Mistress Rugg—turned to other things.

In fact, the missing Ruggs might have been forgotten entirely if people hadn't begun to spot the pair in unlikely places.

In 1820 a New York businessman named Jonathan Dunwell was traveling by stagecoach from Providence, Rhode Island, to Boston. He recalled how their party had seen a flustered, frightened-looking man with a little girl driving a battered rig. The man glared at the stage driver and continued wordlessly on his way.

"Who is that man?" Jonathan asked the driver. "He seems in great trouble."

"Nobody knows who he is, but his person and the child are familiar to me. I have met him more than a hundred times, and have been so often asked the way to Boston by that man—even when he was traveling directly from that town—that of late I have refused any communication with him. And that is the reason he gave me such a fixed look."

"But does he never stop anywhere?" Jonathan inquired.

"I have never known him to stop anywhere longer than to inquire the way to Boston. He will tell you he cannot stay a moment, for he must reach Boston that night."

And to add to the mystery, the driver reported, after each sighting of the lost and lonely couple, a thunderstorm always followed.

Along that same route, Polley's Tavern was also visited by

the bewildered traveler and little girl. The man stopped, inquired the way to Boston, then vanished in the wrong direction.

A tin-pan peddler reported meeting the mysterious pair in the early 1800s. Four meetings, in fact, and in four different states. Each time, the exhausted-looking man asked the way to Boston as the frightened little girl clung to his arm. "I wish never to see that man and horse again," the peddler said. "They do not look to me as though they belong to this world."

It was not long after a few such reports that people began to realize that the missing Peter Rugg and his daughter were still around. And speculation soon began that they had been recast in some form other than human. It was as though they had been misplaced in time and space and were continually searching—unsuccessfully—for that well-known route that would deliver them home to Boston.

## A FICKLE ROADWAY

*Boston shifts with the wind, and playsall around the compass. One man tells meit is to the east, another to the west; and the guide-posts too, they all point the wrong way.*

—Peter Rugg

Sightings continued after the Revolutionary War.

A guest at Bennett's Hotel in Hartford, Connecticut, spotted the displaced pair. "He looks wet and weary, and farther from Boston than ever," the man said.

Over the years there were many chance encounters with the man and girl. Each event had two things in common: The man would invariably ask the way to Boston, and the rendezvous would always occur during or immediately after a torrential rainstorm.

The people most likely to see the Ruggs where those who spent a lot of time on the roads: peddlers, stage drivers, vagabonds, mail carriers.

The toll taker on the Charlestown Bridge had a number of run-ins. Each occurred during a rainstorm. In every event Peter refused to stop and pay the toll. Once, greatly angered by the repeated gate crashing, the toll man hurled his stool at Peter's horse as it thundered by. To his horror, the stool passed silently through the animal and smashed against the guardrail on the far side of the bridge.

Adonariah Adams, a rotund and genial man, was for many years the driver of the Portland Mail. In 1860 he reported seeing Peter Rugg in the vicinity of Newburyport, Massachusetts. Mr. Adams's testimony is recorded as follows:

> I noticed thunderheads in the southern sky and whipped the horses into a trot. Ahead of us, heavy streaks of lightning flashed across the horizon and I realized that we were in for a nasty tempest.
>
> We ascended Witch-Hang Hill at a fast clip and as we reached the top, something compelled me to look back. There I saw Peter Rugg's carriage tearing after us and gaining fast. My horses took fright and began to run at a desperate and dangerous pace, but Rugg's great beast steadily gained until he was racing neck and neck with my wheel-horses.
>
> Suddenly, a bolt of lightning struck the Rugg conveyance. In the instantaneous flash, I saw Peter and his daughter glowing with fire like a horseshoe as it is taken from the blacksmith's hearth. At the same time, flames and sparks cascaded from the mouth and ears of the huge bay horse and I was almost stifled by the odor of brimstone, yet

the bolt seemed to have no effect on the creature for that carriage continued on. My horses were so frightened that they leaped from the road, wrecking the coach against a boulder.

Perhaps Mr. Adams was the first to articulate what many had suspected. "It is my opinion," he said, "that what I saw was the Devil's shade of Peter Rugg."

*Have the rivers, too, changed their courses, as the cities have changed places?*

–Peter Rugg

The earthly search for Peter Rugg had been abandoned long before the year 1800. But the encounters continued. Many people guessed that the Ruggs' seemingly endless journey had something to do with that last defiant utterance reported by Tom Cutter back in 1770: "I will see home tonight in spite of storm or the Devil. Or may I never see home!"

As Adonariah Adams speculated, "I have heard it asserted that Heaven sometimes sets a mark on a man, either for judgment or a trial. Under which Peter Rugg now labours, I cannot say; therefore I am rather inclined to pity than to judge."

## HELL TO PAY

One of the last well-documented sightings of Peter and Jenny Rugg occurred in the early twentieth century. A minister named Rev. Samuel Nickles was traveling from the village of Wickford, Rhode Island, toward Providence. En route, the preacher and his horse were caught in a wicked thunderstorm. The cleric hunched his shoulders against the downpour, hoping—perhaps praying—he would find shelter when he reached Quonset.

When the Reverend Nickles heard the sound of a rapidly approaching carriage, he looked up from the muddy roadbed, squinting into the rain. A rig was racing toward him at an incautious pace. A pale, terrified-looking man was at the reins. Beside him a little girl clung with both hands to his cloak.

There was no room to avoid a collision on the narrow road. "Stop!" cried the panicking pastor. "Stop!"

The Reverend Nickles's horse reared up in fear, throwing the frightened clergyman to the ground, where he remained unconscious until a passerby discovered him in the morning.

The reverend staggered a bit, steadying himself by resting his hand against a nearby stone. On its surface he and his companion were startled to see the shape of a cloven hoof literally seared into the hard rock.* The reverend hurriedly left the area. When he told the tale, people became more convinced than ever that Peter Rugg and his innocent daughter were somehow at the mercy of the Devil.

## THE END AT LAST?

Repeated sightings of Peter Rugg and his daughter are too numerous to chronicle here. Seemingly doomed to travel forever, the couple have been spotted in every New England state, all the way to the Canadian border, and as far away as Concord, Virginia. They are always sighted just before or during a heavy rainstorm. They refuse to tarry long, restricting their conversation to simple variations on "Which way to Boston?"

[*Michael Bell, Rhode Island folklorist, tells me that Devil's Foot Rock, near Quonset, is still there. He says, 'The road 'improvement' project has made the rock even more difficult to see, but it is just to the west of Post Road and just south of Devil's Foot Road.']

Beginning before the Revolutionary War and continuing until well after, it seems that Peter and Jenny were somehow knocked out of the fragile alignment of space and time. They are occasionally visible to us; we can be visible to them. But for some reason our two worlds can never become aligned for long.

*Here is evidently a conspiracy against me; alas, I shall never see Boston! The highways refuse me a passage, the rivers change their courses, and there is no faith in the compass.*

–Peter Rugg

Peter Rugg is invariably reported as looking pretty much the same from sighting to sighting, though it may be inferred that he appears more exhausted and maniacal as the years pass. In his increasing frustration, he simply cannot find his way home. Nor can he return to that time before the Revolution: the colonial Boston that he seeks. Apparently he is cursed to wander, without aging, without resting, without comfort or company beyond that provided by the terrified child at his side.

But over the decades the descriptions of Jenny have changed. While her father doesn't seem to age, some reports imply that Jenny has grown from little girl to aged crone as their trek through time continues.

Of late there have not been many reports. It is likely Peter Rugg avoids the superhighways, the paved roads, the unfamiliar thoroughfares that, because of their strangeness to him, most surely will not lead to Boston.

If he is sighted today, it will be on the back roads of New England, the unpaved, rutted rural routes that crisscross our Yankee Kingdom, leading everywhere but home.

~

## AUTHOR'S NOTE

The story of Peter Rugg has been told for about 200 years. Oral storytellers and writers—fiction and nonfiction—recognize its extraordinary power. It is like a hybrid of Paul Revere's ride, blended with the saga of the Flying Dutchman and the story of the Wandering Jew.

It has appeared in print regularly, in many versions. Nathaniel Hawthorne picked up on it in his story "A Virtuoso's Collection" (1846) and again, thematically, in "Ethan Brand" (1850). In 1883 it appeared in Samuel Adams Drake's *New England Legends and Folk Lore,* and in 1890 it was published in *The Yankee Blade,* an eight-page illustrated newspaper.

More recently, I read a version in *Yankee Magazine* (circa 1960) and saw *Yankee's* article reprinted in the Austin N. Stevens–edited volume *Mysterious New England* (1971). Most recently I enjoyed Holly Mascott Nadler's retelling in her entertaining book *Ghosts of Boston Town* (2002).

The story of Peter Rugg, like its central character, has done a good bit of traveling. Somewhere along the way it left the printed page to firmly lodge itself in the oral tradition where—though modified endlessly to fit the style of individual storytellers—it has been passed along as fact, scaring generation after generation.

Massachusetts poet Amy Lowell wrote of the fear it inspired in her: "How often have I driven through the hush which precedes a thunderstorm, all of a tremble lest I should meet the old man in the yellow-wheeled chaise." In 1917 she used it in her narrative "Before the Storm" in the *North American Review.*

Another poet, Louise Imogen Guiney, was also familiar with the story, casting it into an 1891 poem of her own, "Peter Rugg, the Bostonian" in *Scribner's Magazine.*

Over the years I've come across it so frequently that I came to accept it as one of New England's most venerable—and true—ghost stories. For me, as well as many others, Peter Rugg became a real person. He made that rare leap from fiction to fact, as did Conan Doyle's Sherlock Holmes, who still receives requests for assistance addressed to his imaginary Baker Street apartment.

In putting together this book, I was eager to include the Peter Rugg saga. As effective as many of the tellings have been, what the aforementioned sources routinely fail to do is disclose exactly where the story came from. In researching this chapter, I discovered its origins.

Though the original manuscript is apparently lost, Peter Rugg began life as a short story, one of the earliest works of American supernatural fiction. It came out in three installments between 1824 and 1827 in a Boston Masonic periodical called *New England Magazine*.

Almost immediately (that same year, 1824) it was reprinted in *The New England Galaxy*. There, fiction and nonfiction were published side by side, with nothing to distinguish one from the other. It was at this point, no doubt, that Peter Rugg began his transformation from literary fiction to legitimate phantom.

The name of the author, Jonathan Dunwell, proved to be the pseudonym for William Austin, a Harvard-educated lawyer and writer. He got his proper attribution in 1841 when the piece was republished in *The Boston Book*. As a literary contrivance, the story is elegant and complicated, clearly the work of a well-educated wordsmith. Some obvious givaways can be pointed out without going into lengthy (and irrelevant) analysis.

The story of Peter Rugg took place before the Revolution. That's also when Paul Revere took his immortal ride. Check the similarity of initials.

Peter Rugg was Dutch. So was the Flying Dutchman, the sea captain who swore during a hurricane that he'd take his ship around the dangerous Cape of Good Hope, even if it took all eternity to do so. Dutchman Peter Rugg swore he'd get his land-bound vessel home despite the terrible storm.

Within the Puritan confines of Peter Rugg's (and William Austin's) era, both Dutchmen were guilty of blasphemy. They challenged divine order—imposed their own wills, rather than God's (which, of course, was undisclosed to them). They *promised* when they should have *prayed,* and were cursed in consequence, condemned to wander sea and land, perhaps till doomsday.

The story of Peter Rugg, fiction though it may be, is a wonderful example of how man can curse himself. And in so doing, make helpless victims of the innocents around him—like his eternally faithful daughter Jenny.

# CONNECTICUT'S VILLAGE OF THE DAMNED

*Something—some malevolent spirit, some terrible ill-fortune—dogged the village's every step forward, until, in the period following the Civil War, that unknown "something" began to catch up with the little town. None could reverse—or adequately explain—the decline and fall of the once proud village at the end of the nineteenth century.*

—David E. Philips, *Legendary Connecticut*

## DEADLY TOWN

Dudleytown is a 2-mile-square plateau in the southwestern part of Cornwall. Its scattering of legend-infested ruins long ago earned it the designation *ghost town*, but—if you believe the stories—*demon town* might be a more accurate description.

"Probably it's the spookiest place in New England," observes writer Robert Ellis Cahill.

There is no shortage of theories to explain why the town was abandoned. Some claim it shouldn't have been built in the first place—that despite its natural beauty, the area couldn't support a population: The land was poor, rocky, too far from navigable water or highways, and way too mountainous. Others blame progress, saying the opening of the West and the growth of urban industry lured the town's population away.

But a growing contingent of believers argue that such rational explanations simply cannot account for the ongoing excess of tragedies that befell Dudleytown. Their paranormal explanations may at first seem naive, simplistic, or superstitious. For Dudleytown, they maintain, is a cursed town, though the source of that curse is still a matter of debate.

Did the first settlers experience a head-on collision with Native American magic? After all, they built their town on Mohawk land. Did the power of shamanistic sorcery seek to repossess Indian hunting grounds?

And there are those who argue that the problem is in the name itself–*Dudley*. If that is so, the curse is English, not American, and long predates the arrival of the first Dudley on North American soil.

Whatever the source, disasters of every description rained down upon the people of Dudleytown. There was no way to predict whom the curse would strike, and no apparent means of escaping its trajectory. It afflicted those who held their ground, and pursued many who tried to run away. In its wake, history records a trail of deaths, ruined lives, and escalating madness.

## THE NAME OF DUDLEY

Those who favor the "Cursed Family" explanation say the trouble started with Sir Edmund Dudley, who'd been accused of stealing money from the royal treasury. On August 18, 1510, by order of King Henry VIII, Sir Edmund was beheaded in London.

Subsequently Edmund's son John, duke of Northumberland, conspired to control the English throne. He conceived a two-step plan: First, he would effect a marriage between his son Guilford and Lady Jane Grey (Henry VII's great-granddaughter). Second, he and his brother Robert, earl of Leicester, would

persuade dying King Edward to pass the crown to his daughter-in-law, Lady Jane.

Power seemed within John's grasp.

But it wasn't to be. Lady Jane did become queen, briefly, but the Dudley machinations were discovered, and all concerned were sentenced to death. Sir John was executed in 1553. Five months later Lady Jane and her husband, Guilford Dudley, were beheaded. Although Robert was ultimately pardoned, he was never free of royal scrutiny.

But perhaps another of Sir John's sons was responsible for the most devastating Dudley assault on England. Returning from a military assignment in France, he brought the plague with him, spreading deadly infection to thousands of his countrymen. Military losses alone weakened the empire.

So through maliciousness, malfeasance, misjudgment, and mistake, the Dudleys had acquired a bad reputation in their homeland. No doubt many individuals cursed their name. But the wrath of a Divine Right Monarch was considered powerful enough to lay a curse all by itself.

It seems that when William Dudley, a direct descendant of Sir John's brother Robert, set out (circa 1639) for what he hoped would be the safety of the New World, he brought the Dudley Curse to America, just as his ancestor brought the plague to England.

## CORNWALL

Starting around 1747, William's three great-grandsons—Abiel, Barzillai, and Gideon—began buying land and settling on some undeveloped acres in Cornwall, Connecticut. By sheer force of numbers, the name *Dudley* stuck to the area; it became known as Dudleytown.

The brothers, and the growing influx of neighbors, subsisted by hunting, raising crops, and logging. Families with such names as *Jones, Carter, Tanner, Patterson,* and more, pitched in and pushed back the dense and undisturbed forest.

When settlers in nearby Salisbury discovered iron, the residents of Dudleytown felled their seemingly endless supply of pine, oak, maple, and chestnut to feed the insatiable furnaces.

And the town flourished for a while, producing a fair number of notable citizens. Mary Cheney married *New York Tribune* publisher and presidential candidate Horace Greeley. Selectman Dcn. Thomas Porter moved to Vermont to become a supreme court judge. His son, Ebenezer, became the respected president of Andover Seminary.

But for every success, the Curse found a victim.

Insanity seized Abiel Dudley. He ended up the local pauper, overseen by a custodian. This once respected town father died an impoverished madman, his suffering prolonged until the unheard-of age of ninety.

Abiel's brother Barzillai predeceased him, dying a peculiar death: He was cut to pieces by savage attackers that may—or may not—have been human.

Brother Gideon—perhaps sensibly—left the area and seems to have vanished from history.

OTHER POSSIBILITIES

But if it were a *family curse*—a curse on the Dudley name and lineage—why did misfortune not restrict its reach only to Dudleys? And why did the town's woes not end with the death of the last Dudley in Dudleytown?

Perhaps we should look to the land for an explanation of Dudleytown's demise. Although there is no known record of its utterance, many people speculate that some unknown shaman's imprecation guaranteed that Dudleytown would never prosper. In the annals of Native American wizardry, there are many examples of such curses.

This may well explain why the Curse touched more than just the Dudley clan, and why distressing events ultimately disabled the town, infecting citizen after citizen like an unholy contagion.

For example, in 1759, when Nathaniel Carter bought the house formerly owned by Abiel Dudley, he may have purchased more than he bargained for. We do not know if misfortune caused the Carters to leave town, but four years later, when the family relocated to Binghamton, New York, ill luck followed. First, one of Nathaniel's children died of a mysterious illness. In October 1764 hostile Indians killed his wife and their youngest son, kidnapped the three remaining children, then torched the house. Though he was away at the time, Nathaniel didn't escape the slaughter. Returning home, he was attacked and hacked to pieces.

Some years later two of his abducted daughters were recovered, but they remained sickly and mad until death. The fate of the third is unknown. She either perished in the wilds or remained an "unredeemed captive," choosing to make her home with the Indians.

Back in Dudleytown, the family of Nathaniel Carter's brother Adoniram also suffered a strange fate. In 1774 some nameless contagion struck down every one of the Carters, touching no one else in town.

Then, in 1813, a less-focused but equally unidentified epidemic indiscriminately wiped out scores of Dudleytown residents, including many members of the pioneering families.

Later, native daughter Mary Greeley supposedly hanged herself a few days before her husband, Horace, lost the presidential election of 1872. Horace, suffering great disappointment and a double loss, degenerated rapidly and died insane on November 29 of the same year.

Also in 1892, a man named Gershon Hollister was murdered in William Tanner's Dudleytown home. William, the only possible suspect, denied the crime but couldn't explain the incident. Apparently the rigors of the resulting investigation proved too much for him, and he, too, succumbed to madness, railing on about demons and ghosts and asserting that Gershon Hollister had been savaged by some awesome, unknown beast. William Tanner remained in this tortured state for far too many years. He passed away at the impossible age of 104, finally ending his prolonged suffering.

In April 1804 a freak bolt of lightning killed Gen. Herman Swift's wife as she stood on her porch. Though the general had been a Revolutionary War hero and adviser to George Washington, the resulting grief drove him into irreversible dementia.

The Curse seemed to touch every family in Dudleytown. Deaths came in unprecedented numbers. Madness claimed more than its fair share of victims. As word spread, frightened residents abandoned their homes and belongings and fled. Not surprisingly, no new families moved in until, by the late nineteenth century, there was only one citizen left in Dudleytown. A solitary Polish immigrant perceived opportunity in the abandoned homes and neglected farmland and settled into the old Rogers place. He worked hard raising sheep but, mercifully, loneliness touched him before he was seized by madness. When he evacuated, Dudleytown was sounding its death rattle.

## BROPHY'S LAST STAND

Then, in 1892, an Irishman named Patrick Brophy heard about the deserted town and decided to take his pick of the empty houses and abandoned belongings. He was heard to state publicly that he feared no man, beast, wild animal, or ghost. That seemed to cover just about everything . . . but not the Curse.

Patrick Brophy moved in with his wife, two sons, and a flock of sheep in tow. Rapid-fire misfortunes met him immediately. His sheep died, his sons vanished, and consumption killed his wife.

The Irishman, like the Pole before him, stood alone determined to conquer the wilderness. But Pat Brophy was forced out when a mysterious fire destroyed his house and everything he owned. If that wasn't enough, a week later he stumbled into Cornwall. Haggard, tattered, wild-eyed, and wan, he raved maniacally about giant animals with cloven hooves and the ghastly green spirits that had chased and tried to capture him.

## A NEW CENTURY BEGINS

Dudleytown should have died then, but it didn't. The Curse—or whatever it is—waited patiently amid the dark, owl-haunted woodland for its next victim.

Around the turn of the twentieth century, while touring the scenic back roads of Connecticut, William C. Clarke and his wife, Harriet, discovered the abandoned town. This isolated, romantic spot was just the place they'd always dreamed about, a perfect location for their cottage in the country. In 1900 they purchased several hundred acres from the town of Cornwall.

William Clarke was a successful surgeon and professor of medicine at Columbia College of Physicians and Surgeons in New York City. He and his wife enjoyed the outdoors and the simple satisfactions of hunting, fishing, and swimming.

Working weekends, Dr. Clarke cleared a perfect piece of land and built their rustic home from felled hemlock. He and his wife laid pipe to a spring and even fashioned a swimming pool in a brook not far from their home.

Distant neighbors, looking on from afar, hoped this ambitious young couple would remain unmolested. Surely this "Curse" business had come to an end once and for all.

## GATHERING SHADOWS

Then one summer weekend Dr. Clarke got a phone call. An emergency situation summoned him back to the city.

His wife seemed oddly reluctant to let him go. She was unusually quiet as they waited at the train station. "Come back quickly," she repeated. "Promise me you'll come back as quickly as you can." She attributed her nervousness to the fact that she had never spent a night alone at the cabin. After the train pulled out, Harriet Clarke remained on the platform for a long time, a solitary figure staring down the empty tracks.

No one knows what happened while Dr. Clarke was away. But we know he returned within thirty-six hours. And the moment he stepped off the train, he knew something was wrong; his wife wasn't there to meet him.

He hired a ride, then ran through the shadowy woods toward the cabin. There was no sign of life anywhere around. No lights burned inside. Everything was quiet, unnaturally still.

Even the owls were silent.

When he rushed to the door, he found it not only unlocked but slightly ajar as well. Tense, sweating, Dr. Clarke stepped into the dark interior. Then he heard the sounds that would shatter his sleep for the rest of his life. Coming from beyond their bedroom door was the shrill, near-hysterical laughter of one hopelessly insane.

In the brief time that Dr. Clarke was away, his wife had gone irreversibly mad.

## NO END IN SIGHT

So there you have it. That's the whole story, or the foundation of it, anyway.

Was the Dudley family truly cursed? Or was there an evil stain on the land itself—preordained by some shaman's lethal utterance?

Or might there be a third possibility, one more mundane than malevolent?

Maybe the Dudley brothers simply picked a bad place to settle. A place of constant shadows, poor rocky land, and unwholesome water; a place inconvenient to urban centers and industry. The rest, quite possibly is coincidence, suggestion, superstition, and some normal atavistic response to things ancient, unsettling, and apparently dangerous.

It is interesting that Dr. Clarke did not flee from Dudleytown. In fact, he remarried in 1920 and, along with other New York doctors, bought up 850 more acres. In December 1924 they formed the Dark Entry Forest Association, which still owns Dudleytown today. Thus they have turned New England's "Village of the Damned" into a Yankee "Area 51."

Dudleytown is sealed off from all visitors and has become a natural–or supernatural–preserve where Mother Nature is permitted to reclaim all that was taken from her.

AUTHOR'S NOTE

I visited Dudleytown for the first time in the late 1960s, during my college years. I'd heard the story, in perhaps a slightly altered state, from a classmate, Craig. He didn't know all the details, just tantalizing fragments about a New England ghost town populated by real ghosts. Then throw in demons and a curse! Well, we were on our way.

It was an easy trip from Vermont, just a straight drop south on Route 7 from Bennington, directly through Massachusetts, and into Connecticut. We stopped at the town of Cornwall Bridge, the jumping-off place to Dudleytown.

Word wasn't out in those days; Dudleytown wasn't the Mecca of Malevolence it has since become. Visitors were still tolerated. No one warned us away, treated us with icy contempt, or threatened legal action, fines, and arrest.

When we stopped at a local eatery to ask directions, we were treated cordially. In fact, I thought I detected an attitude of bemused tolerance as the man behind the counter sketched a crude map on a paper napkin. (I recall a mild disappointment at the meeting's lack of gothic overtones. Having seen too many horror movies, I'd expected him to spit tobacco juice and mumble something like, "You young fellas hadn't ought to be pokin' around in them wood . . . no sir. Not now, an' 'specially not after dark.")

Anyway, instructions in hand, we quickly discovered the

dirt road entryway to Dudleytown. Access was blocked. Poles were driven into the ground, or there was a gate, or fallen trees, or something. We had to park and walk a long, long way—that I remember very clearly.

Our first chill came when we saw the sign: DARK ENTRY ROAD. Dark Entry? I felt like Dante, abandoning all hope as Virgil guided him into Hades.

Craig preceded me along the shrunken pathway that must once have led directly into the heart of Dudleytown. I imagined the horses and wagons zipping along this ruined road, now bumpy with boulders and crowded with brush—impassable with anything but a four-wheel-drive vehicle, or tank.

Gradually, although it was a midsummer afternoon, we found ourselves in semidarkness. Stranger still, it was as if all sounds had ceased. We felt suddenly colder. The atmosphere was perfect for a good scare as we pressed forward beneath the dense canopy of trees. Dudleytown is positioned amid four mountains, so it is always in shadows, always dark.

Involuntarily, we found ourselves talking in terse whispers. "How do we even know this is the right road?"

"It's gotta be. There's no other roads around."

Shortly after we crossed the first brook, our convictions were confirmed. We spotted an ancient hand-hewn sign that was barely readable and hanging askew. Just like a prop in a horror film. It said—if I'm remembering this correctly—DUDLEY-TOWNE.

I don't think either of us realized how far we would have to hike to reach the intersections of Dark Entry and Dudleytown Roads. Their convergence marked the heart of a village that once was. A village whose last building tumbled into its cellar hole around 1925.

Looking back, I'm not sure exactly what we expected to find there. Cairns? Graves? Pieces of timber? Maybe even an old smelting furnace with scatterings of slag—the artifacts of the extinct village?

We avoided repeating Craig's campfire stories about ghosts and demons as we hiked along the steep road that hugged a perilous ravine. We stumbled often. Once Craig fell. But all the while my mind involuntarily reviewed the unspoken details: Dudleytown is a cursed village. It's haunted. Demon-infested. The original settlers were plagued by weird animals, mysterious disappearances, inexplicable deaths, horrible mutilations, epidemic insanity, and ghastly diabolical confrontations. People died, moved on, or escaped in terror, abandoning their village so nature—or supernature—could reclaim it all.

Something screamed.

We froze, squinted into dark pools of shadows between twisted trees. Then we forced ourselves to laugh.

"Some kind of bird," Craig whispered, his voice pinched an octave too high.

"Sounded like an owl," I said. "A little early for owls, isn't it?"

"Dunno. Pretty dark here."

A machine gun fired.

My pulse quickened to keep pace.

"Pileated woodpecker," Craig said. "That one I know."

Nerves jacked up a notch, we continued on our way, hurrying to get there quickly so we could be gone before sunset.

But get where?

Of course I wasn't expecting a ghost town like the ones I'd seen in western movies, full of brittle, sagging buildings, and tumbleweed. Dry desert air preserves structures. New England's weather digests them.

So what could we expect to see?

I remember passing stone walls—lots of stone walls. And tumbled stone foundations, cellar holes, and other signs of a village's own variety of final corruption. At length, our venture into the unknown was anticlimactic. We didn't meet any ghosts. We saw nary a demon. But with rocket-fueled imaginations intact, we left hurriedly, satisfied that we'd been, delighted to be gone. Had we found the center of town? To this day we don't know. There was no way to tell. In any event, I've never been back. But over the years I've revisited Dudleytown in books, magazines, and newspapers. I've watched it grow from afar, a kind of hideous rebirth.

It was never rebuilt, of course. But it has grown just the same. Its reputation today is probably more far reaching than when it was alive. It has taken on postmortem allure.

Immediately after my circa-1968 visit to Dudleytown, I was able to discover only two written sources that told its tale: Sterry and Garrigus's book *They Found a Way* (1938) and Fessenden Blanchard's *Ghost Towns of New England* (1960).

Three years after my trip, Dudleytown appeared again in Austin N. Stevens's *Mysterious New England* (1971).

The basic story they told hasn't changed much. What's changed is the number of people who've become aware of it. The volume of visitors. And the embellishments those visitors have contributed.

## FANNING THE FLAMES

Today Dudleytown's fame continues to spread.

In 1989 infamous Connecticut demon chasers Ed and Lorraine Warren talked about Dudleytown in their ghostwritten book *Ghost Hunters*. Sharon Jarvis included it in her *Dead Zones* in 1992.

In his August 1993 *Playboy* interview, Hollywood ghostbuster Dan Aykroyd gave Dudleytown a real shot of adrenaline, calling it the "most haunted place on earth." (However, the misinformed mystic moved the town to Massachusetts. No doubt his attempt "to protect the innocent.")

Dudleytown regularly appears in TV scare shows, lurid periodicals, weird Web sites, newspaper Hallowe'en stories, and books such as this. Its true history seems to be lost, replaced by a massive work of fiction, the unintentional collaboration of hundreds of thrill seekers, sensationalist authors, and lazy researchers.

Contemporary trespassers invariably find the place "forbidding." They come away—as Craig and I did—vaguely frightened, often not knowing why. They say they sense something watching them, or they feel unaccountably cold, even on sunny summer days. Others claim more tangible experiences, such as the ill-fated television documentary team that was plagued with equipment failure, personal illness, and ruined film.

The ubiquitous ghost town resides in multiple places on the Web. On the New England Paranormal Web site, a woman identified only as "Sarah from Connecticut" writes of walking along the silent road in 1998 and hearing what "sounded like a huge metal dumpster dragging against asphalt."

Still other explorers report visions of looming dark shapes in the daytime or lights that flicker helter-skelter through the trees at night. And many visitors hear screeching sounds. Owls, perhaps? But more likely a chorus of woodland demons, or the souls of Dudleytown inhabitants who can never escape the site of their earthly demise.

## A WARNING TO THE CURIOUS

The consequence of all this attention is that a *real* curse has befallen the town, a curse bolstered by the 1999 film *The Blair Witch Project*. Somehow, perversely, it made the notion of a haunted woodland immensely inviting, inspiring every self-professed goth and ghost seeker with a self-destructive streak to Dudleytown hoping to ferret out his or her own personal bogeyman—while littering, burning, and vandalizing the Connecticut backcountry.

In short, the annual trickle of Dudleytown's curiosity seekers became a deluge. Hordes of horror hounds with unfathomable agendas descended on the ghost town as if it were a Demonic Disneyland. Bikers, goths, pseudo-psychics, Ouija-toting paranormal investigators, Warren groupies, and all manner of inconsiderate intruders imposed, vandalized, and harassed Cornwall residents. In 2002 police officers were summoned to Dudleytown seventy-nine times, responding to complaints about drinking parties, campfires, littering, disorderly conduct, and vandalism.

Members of the Dark Entry Forest Association placed Dudleytown off limits. Today visitors are the real Curse of Dudleytown. Any legitimate spirits, ghosts, or demons have probably had the good sense to leave.

# NIX'S MATE

*In any case, the verification of innocence, if such it shall be account-
ed, came too late by a century to save Nix's Mate from the halter.*

–Samuel Adams Drake, "Nix's Mate"

## HARBOR TALES

For decades the thirty-seven islands of Boston Harbor were
essentially ignored by the city's population. It is easy to see
why Bostonians might turn a blind eye to, say, Spectacle Island,
which was long used as a horse rendering plant (then, in 1959,
converted to a garbage dump). Islands here could vanish, and
seemingly no one would notice. In fact three of them—Apple,
Governors, and Bird—were gobbled up by Logan airport, and
today no one seems to miss them.

But lately the Boston Harbor islands are being rediscovered
as a handy escape from the oppressions of urban density. Due
largely to the work of writer and folklorist Edward Rowe Snow,
the good people of Boston have finally perceived what has been
right under their noses: a veritable cache of jewels in their
midst, a maritime oasis where they can enjoy camping, hiking,
swimming, and historical exploration without having to travel
very far.

For example, on Castle Island, which protects the entrance
to Boston Harbor, stands Fort Independence. Built in 1835, it is
the oldest continuously used military fortification on the continent.

The Boston Light, North American's first lighthouse, was
erected in 1716 on Little Brewster Island. British troops

destroyed it in 1776, but it was rebuilt in 1783 exactly as we see it today. It is the last staffed lighthouse in North America; all the others are automated.

Archaeological evidence reveals that people have been living on, or at least visiting, these islands for at least 8,000 years. Interestingly, the oldest human skeleton in New England was discovered on Peddocks Island in the 1960s. It is believed to be more than 4,000 years old.

Bones, as we shall see, are an important theme in this chapter. For where there are bones, there is history; and where there is history, there are stories. Edward Rowe Snow collected an abundance of fascinating tales in his book *The Islands of Boston Harbor* (1971), many of them still intriguing today.

For example, scores of people have spotted the ghostly "Lady in Black" at Fort Warren on Georges Island. Her name, Mr. Snow tells us, is Mrs. Lanier. During the Civil War her husband, Andrew, was among the Confederate prisoners housed within the grim confines of the fort. After learning of her husband's incarceration, his youthful bride concocted a daring escape plan. Disguised as a man, Mrs. Lanier managed to enter Fort Warren. But during their escape attempt, she accidentally shot and killed her husband. Sentenced to be hanged for her efforts, she went to the gallows in the black dress of a widow. Today, still wearing black, her ghost haunts the dark interior of Fort Warren and is occasionally spotted walking the grounds.

In 1827 writer Edgar Allan Poe was stationed as a soldier at Fort Independence on Castle Island. While there he heard the lurid tale of a fatal duel between a sadistic officer, Captain Green, and a well-liked lieutenant, Robert F. Massie. After Lieutenant Massie was slain on Christmas Day 1817, his friends took revenge on Captain Green by walling him up alive. His bones were discovered many years later (1905) shackled to the floor and wearing the tattered remains of an ancient army officer's uniform. Mr. Poe turned these events into a lurid tale of his own—"The Cask of Amontillado."

But stories of spirits and revenge are not what interest us here. We're considering curses, and among the Boston islands we find one that involves bones and an executed seaman's unique retribution—the Curse of Nix's Mate.

## A CURSED ISLE

Unlike most curse stories—which are typically embellished and added to by generations of tellers—with each passing decade a bit more of the tale of Nix's Mate is lost. Sadly, it, like its namesake, is in danger or disappearing altogether. As far back as 1884, historian Samuel Adams Drake placed it among New England's "lost legends."

We'll try to ferret out enough of the details to record the story one last time, though I fear we'll have to secure certain of its building blocks with the mortar of imagination.

We know that in the old days it was the custom to erect a public gibbet at the entrance of certain New England towns. The grotesque practice is so outdated that today some may not recall the meaning of the term.

A *gibbet* was an upright post with a T-shaped crosspiece used to display the corpses of executed criminals. This repulsive exhibit of medieval signage was intended to warn newcomers about the consequence of misbehavior. As Mr. Drake says in his *New England Legends and Folk Lore,* "It followed that the stranger who passed underneath one of these ensigns of terror could have no doubt that he had entered a Christian land, since the administration of justice according to its most civilized forms confronted him upon its very threshold."

In the case of Boston Town, one entrance was by sea, so it was routine to hang the chained bodies of pirates and other maritime malefactors at the entrance to the port, signaling a similar warning to those whose highway was aquatic.

Nix's Mate is one of two Boston Harbor islands that have long evoked a sense of tragedy and terror for having hosted these cruel rituals. The other is the aforementioned Bird Island. Between the pair, more than fifteen notorious pirates were tried, condemned, then hanged for their bloody deeds. Afterward, their corpses were strung up on the gibbet and left to rot until their sun-bleached bones fell, cracked into pieces, and littered the land below.

That much we know for sure.

We also know that Nix's Mate was once owned by John Gallop, a Boston merchant whose name still identifies the adjacent Gallops Island. When he acquired both in 1636, the smaller island was called Nix's Mate, and so we may assume the tragedy that inspired its name occurred sometime before that. We may also assume there was once a Captain Nix and that he had a mate (mate, that is, in the seafaring sense).

According to surviving data and local belief, the bones of Captain Nix's mate are among those that have turned to dust on the island. For Captain Nix was one of those cruel and tyrannical sea captains whose harsh orders and ready whip inspired so many able seamen to rebel. Exactly what ignited the mutiny is unrecorded, but Captain Nix was murdered at sea and the mutineers took over his ship.

Their freedom was short-lived. They were quickly taken into custody.

Then as now, rebellion at sea is punishable by death. And when the conspirators were brought in for judgment, they all had their story ready: Each in turn blamed the first mate. It was he who organized the mutiny. It was he who murdered the captain.

Captain Nix's mate—whose name, unfortunately, is lost at sea—was in effect accused of the crime on hearsay evidence. He was tried, convicted, and sentenced in Boston, then boated out into the harbor for execution.

The small crowd of witnesses assembled there on that windy morning were at first unsympathetic to his protests of innocence. They'd heard it all before. Even the most bloodthirsty freebooter or cutthroat would typically proclaim he'd been wrongly convicted.

But this young man was so earnest, so plaintive, and so apparently honest that certain spectators began to question the judgment. After all, his record was unblemished; his service had been loyal. And if the crew—a scurvy lot at best—would murder the captain, wouldn't they just as readily frame the mate, especially if so doing would save their own necks?

Despite growing doubts, the order was given to proceed with the execution.

"I am innocent," the mate repeated, and—standing tall and straight—he steadfastly continued to assert his innocence until the end.

But those were not his final words.

Before the executioner tightened the noose, Nix's mate laid a curse designed to demonstrate proof of his innocence. From the gallows he shouted, "Because you royal magistrates have hanged an innocent man, this place of execution—this ghastly isle—will be destroyed. Mark my words, for they will ensure that no such abomination of justice can ever occur here again."

With that the hangman's rope jerked taut.

## A WATERY GRAVE

Since that day the waves have done their work. The sea's salty tongue has argued constantly for the mate's innocence, persistently lapping away at what was once an island of several acres. An island thereafter called Nix's Mate.

Over the years, every trace of the soil to which the bones of hanging victims were consigned has disappeared. Today Nix's Mate has all but vanished. Only a solitary monument—a high cement pyramid channel marker atop blackened boulders—indicates the whereabouts of this grisly graveyard of the sea.

## AUTHOR'S NOTE

It speaks well of this forgotten seaman, strengthens his case for innocence, that he did not use his deathbed curse to harm his accusers and executioners before he was swung off into eternity. Instead, he spoke out against an imperfect justice system, then wished away, via cursing, its means of execution.

While the story of Nix's Mate works well as a parable, there is no legitimate history that supports the story of the curse or the hanging. True, the island has, for the most part, disappeared. I hope that long after it has returned completely to the sea, the story of Nix's Mate—this version or some other—will still be told.

# THAT OLD
# SAND FARM

*The sand did not relent. After killing the farm flora, it played a waiting game with the healthy timbers that bordered the fields. It crept over the tree roots and settled in layers until the trees bent over and died. The wind made an eerie sound, whistling through all the dead trees.*

—Carol Olivieri Schulte, *Ghosts on the Coast of Maine*

## A BLASTED HEATH

Near Freeport, Maine—close to the ocean, but closer still to a thriving tourist community, complete with L. L. Bean, Ralph Lauren, and Banana Republic outlets—is a mysterious arid wasteland, a bleak panorama of sun-blasted sand that covers nearly a hundred acres of once fertile soil.

There is no question that this Saharan vista used to be a flourishing farm: Peaks of buildings protrude from wind-driven dunes. Half-buried shacks and ancient wagons emerge and vanish as the sandy tide ebbs and flows. Gnarled treetops—appearing now like stunted shrubbery—distend from gritty drifts below which blueberries once grew and cattle grazed.

Yet this blighted island of sand is surrounded by perfectly healthy vegetation; lush green trees and leafy bushes are visible in every direction.

Something obviously happened here . . . something that transformed fertile farmland into the bewildering wilderness now known as the "Desert of Maine."

So what was it?

Meteor crash?

Weapons testing?

Atomic warfare?

Most geologists will tell you it's the result of bad nine-teenth-century farming practices. They'll talk about improper crop rotation. They'll tell how sheep, cattle, and goats overgrazed on a thin coating of topsoil. Sheep, they'll say, were particularly destructive, pulling out clumps of sod and destroying the protective layer of grass that kept the dunes at bay.

But Maine author Carol Olivieri Schulte gives a darker explanation: This Down East desert, she maintains, is the result of deception, betrayal, and ultimately . . . a curse.

In Ms. Schulte's unique and imaginative version of the story, she maintains that it all began back in 1797 when Maine was still part of Massachusetts. Thomas Grayson and his wife, Elizabeth, acquired the farm, worked their 300 acres, and began to build a family.

As was so routinely the tragedy of early farm life, Elizabeth died young, leaving Thomas to raise their three fine sons alone. In time the two oldest brothers followed the well-trodden path that led so many Maine lads to the sea. But the youngest son, David, remained with his father.

After a respectable amount of time, Thomas Grayson remarried. His bride was a local widow named Hattie. Possibly it was a marriage of love, but the era and situation suggest it was more likely one of convenience.

Hattie had a son of her own, Jonas, so immediately after the wedding, the two moved into the Grayson farmhouse. The land was generous in those days and could easily sustain all four members of the new family.

Everything went well until 1836, when Thomas—who was getting on in years—took sick. His health degenerated rapidly.

Soon it became clear that he would never recover.

Before passing on, he exacted a deathbed promise from his wife. He made Hattie swear to turn the farm over to Thomas's son, the hardworking David.

She said she would, allowing her husband to pass on with an easy mind.

But she lied.

She delivered the Grayson farm to her own son, Jonas.

Understandably feeling betrayed, David Grayson left, forfeiting his home to the conniving pair. Then, some months later, Hattie noticed a small pile of sand near the barn. It wasn't a very big pile—only about the size of an overturned mixing bowl. But it was mysterious. Where had it come from?

After a week, she noticed that the tiny mound seemed to be growing. Now there was enough to fill a bucket.

In a couple of months, the bucket had become a dune. And the dune grew, spreading uncontrollably like flowing masses of crystallized lava.

Makeshift blockades proved useless.

Prayer failed.

In time the sandy tide overran everything. It killed trees, ruined machinery, and permanently immobilized the wagon. By the end of the decade, only the top floor of the barn and roof of the springhouse remained visible.

Around 1860 Hattie became ill. Exhausted, fragile, and afraid, she left this sandy plain for the greener pastures of the spirit world.

Jonas stayed alone, becoming more eccentric and befuddled as the accumulating sand grew into dunes more than 70 feet high. In 1875 the solitary survivor gave up. Now an old man without resources, Jonas moved on and was lost to history.

## GOLDRUP'S GOLD

The farm remained dormant until 1917, when the enterprising Henry Goldrup saw Maine's mysterious desert and imagined an oil well. He bought the land and began to exploit its unique characteristics. First he decided to manufacture cement—but the sand proved too fine to hold concrete blocks together.

Next he considered the possibility of glass production, but the sand's high mica content made Henry's glass smoky, black, and useless.

Just when it seemed that his efforts, too, would be cursed, Henry got a brainstorm. He stuck out a sign that said DESERT OF MAINE, and charged ten cents per person to see it. Thus, in 1920, one of Maine's most successful tourist attractions was born. In a way Henry Goldrup *had* struck oil—the petroleum that fueled America's booming automotive tourism brought wealth directly to him.

Sure, he had some inconveniences, but nothing of curse-like proportions. Sarah, the camel he imported to entertain visitors, had an unfriendly disposition. When she began spitting at tourists, Henry packed her off to the nearest zoo. And the stubborn little donkeys he used to transport visitors regularly went on strike and bolted back to the comfort of their barn.

Nonetheless, Henry Goldrup ran his sand farm for more than sixty years. And Maine's strange desert has continued to thrive to this day—a blessing born from a curse.

~

## AUTHOR'S NOTE

But, we must wonder, was there ever really a curse at all?

Freeport's historical records reveal nothing about Thomas Grayson, his son David, or the treacherous team of Hattie and Jonas. Apparently they never existed.

History says the Desert of Maine began as the Tuttle Farm. That in 1797 William Tuttle moved his family, house and all, to the 300-acre site that was then as promising and prosperous looking as any other Maine farmland.

For years he successfully grew potatoes, vegetables, and hay. He established an apple orchard, kept a herd of cattle, and raised a large family. Within three generations, however, the Tuttles' farm was overgrazed. The topsoil gradually disappeared, uncovering an ancient and massive deposit of sand. Slowly the newfound desert spread, and in despair the Tuttles surrendered, leaving their desert to its destiny.

It is likely William cursed his luck more than once. But if his bad luck wasn't attributable to a curse, we're forced to ask the same question posed by the fictitious Hattie Grayson and the historical William Tuttle: Where did all the sand come from?

Well, as Maine humorist Tim Sample so succinctly put it, "When all else fails, blame it on a glacier."

And that, precisely, is the culprit. Geologists say that 11,000 years ago, at the end of the last ice age, a glacier slid through and deposited vast quantities of pulverized sand and minerals. Glacial till has become the Desert of Maine.

Since 2004 the present owners, Ginger and Gary Currens, have continued the tourist tradition. And the sand dunes—little by little—continue to grow.

# No Mercy from Mercie Dale

*But for the Haydens, all is past.*
*Their fortune vanished with the family name.*

–Louis A. Lamoureux, "Fall of the House of Hayden"

## THE FIRST GENERATION

On February 20, 1927, a frail and sickly old woman died, totally alone and penniless, in a ramshackle farmhouse in Waterville, Maine. With her death a family had "daughtered out"–for she was the last of the line. And the New England dynasty of William Hayden vanished forever from the face of the earth.

As villagers laid her in the ground, they also laid to rest a curse that had taken more than a century to run its fatal course.

Today all that remains of the once powerful Haydens is a grand brick mansion just outside Albany, Vermont, a collection of elegant tombstones, and a cycle of terrifying tales involving spirits, maledictions, and revenge from beyond the grave.

## IN THE BEGINNING . . .

Events began in Braintree, Massachusetts, in 1798, not long after the Revolutionary War, when William Hayden married Silence Dale.

William was an energetic young man with a pioneering spirit. He still carried in his makeup the English notion that the more land a man possesses, the more power he wields. Dreams of wealth and distinction beckoned him into the untamed expanse of wilderness at the northern fringes of the newly established nation.

With wife Silence and Mercie Dale—her wealthy widowed mother—in tow, William traveled up the Connecticut River and along the Hazen Military Road until they reached the sparsely populated Craftsbury, Vermont.

There William erected a simple log cabin, but this was to be but a temporary stopover. The shrewd and ambitious settler speculated that greater opportunities awaited 10 miles farther north, in the unexploited wilds near Canada.

Using money he'd borrowed from his mother-in-law, William purchased Lot Number 4 in an unpopulated township called Lutterloh—today's Albany, Vermont. He constructed a modest frame house, the first to be built there. At its completion, the three of them traveled by oxcart to their new home. This was not the first time William Hayden had borrowed money from Mercie Dale. She was in the habit of helping the young couple during troubled times, and there were many such instances as the three of them resettled. But William had promised to provide for the aging widow, and there was something contagious in his unwavering optimism.

Between 1801 and 1804 William's energy and persuasiveness established him as one of Lutterloh's founding fathers. He became the official surveyor as the town was portioned out. Rather than accepting payment for his work, William took extra land as compensation. He opened up a modest tavern and the first store in town. Eventually he founded a spinning and weaving mill, where he offered employment to women from the village.

His apparent public-spiritedness won him a position as town selectman. He was also elected captain of the local militia. Perhaps his crowning achievement was to get himself named the area's first (and only) customs officer. This made it easy for him to move goods in and out of Canada. Eventually, however, accusations of cattle smuggling lost him the appointment. With that, the first conspicuous public shadow was cast over William Hayden's seemingly sterling character.

But through all his trials and triumphs, William's primary motivation was acquiring land. His holdings increased far beyond Lot Number 4 until, by 1823, he was dangerously overextended and in serious financial straits.

Once again he turned to his mother-in-law, Mercie Dale, to ask for money.

Over the years he had borrowed a considerable sum from her—the exact total is not known—but even in times of plenty, he had neglected to pay her back.

That he had provided for her was expected behavior from a dutiful son-in-law: That was "family." But the loans were something else again: business.

This time Mercie put her foot down. She knew how he'd been dealing with her, and she had observed his questionable dealings with men in the area.

This time Mercie Dale said no. There would be no more loans.

In the months that followed, William continued to badger her, reminding Mercie that her continued well-being, and that of her daughter, depended on his meeting his financial obligations. And—he never failed to reiterate—he would eventually pay back every cent when his fortune was certain.

By now Mercie Dale's view of her son-in-law had changed. She held firmly to her purse strings and parried his every argument. She would advance him no more money. As he persisted,

Mercie's bitterness and suspicion grew, and tension escalated in the Hayden household. In time the old woman began to feel ill. When her condition did not improve, another realization came to her: If she were to die, *all* her money would become William's.

Months passed and her health got no better. Now she began to suspect that William might be poisoning her. Her daughter, Silence, assured Mercie that no such thing was happening, but the tenaciousness of Mercie's illness argued to the contrary.

Finally she overtly accused William of trying to kill her. Despite his protests, Mercie Dale summoned what strength she had left and moved out of the Hayden house. She had arranged to take a room in the home of her friend and neighbor Sally Rogers.

But before she left the Hayden property, with William and Silence standing by, Mercie Dale articulated the curse that would eventually lead to the family's destruction. She said, "The Hayden name shall die in the third generation, and the last to bear the name shall die in poverty."

Exactly what empowered the Widow Dale to make such a proclamation, and why she chose to defer its effects for three generations, remains a topic for speculation. Presumably she wanted to spare her daughter immediate discomfort while wiping William, and all his progeny, off the face of the earth.

In any case, not long afterward, from the effects of poison, or from disappointment, or possibly from the ravages of some undiagnosed illness or the rigors of frontier life, Mercie Dale passed away. She was buried in the Rogers family cemetery, where her remains would be nowhere near the final resting place of the family she'd cursed and abandoned.

## BEYOND MERCIE

After Mercie's death, William's luck began to change.

His shady financial wheelings and dealings started to catch up with him. By 1830 neighbors to whom he owed money were filing lawsuit after lawsuit against him. He lost every one.

Before he could skip town to avoid his creditors, he was "sworn out" by the community. In effect, they banished him. William moved farther north, crossing the border into Potton, Quebec. While he was enjoying legal immunity in a foreign country, he got into political trouble by making ill-advised remarks against the British monarchy. As officials hauled him off to a Montreal jail, he somehow escaped. He fled south across the border and finally settled in Farnsworth, New York, where, in 1846 he died a poor and broken man.

Perhaps—at the very end—William's thoughts were of the nine children he'd fathered with Silence. Of them, only one son and one daughter had reached adulthood. When he died at age sixty-nine, William Hayden might well have believed Mercie Dale's curse was starting to work . . .

## MAKING A STAND

Having remained in Albany, two Hayden children lived to maturity: Arathuza, the daughter, and William. Arathuza died unmarried and childless at age sixty-four.

When William Jr.—known as Will—reached thirty years of age, he was determined to make a stand in the community that had rejected his father. His mother, Silence, joined him there after her husband's death.

Silence—like so many citizens of Albany, Vermont—was to live to a remarkably old age. In 1872 she passed away at age ninety-four. During that time she saw her son, Will, become a rich and powerful man.

At the time of her death, he ordered the village church bell tolled. That sound announcing the passing of Silence Dale marked the end of the first generation of Haydens.

## THE SECOND GENERATION

Will's plan was to carry on, perhaps redeem, the family name. Among his many motivations, no doubt, was the specter of his grandmother and the curse she had uttered. Could it be the reason all his brothers and sisters had died prematurely? Could it have caused the reversal of his father's luck?

Well, he thought, with strength and determination, even that can be conquered. By God he *would* perpetuate the family name, and in a manner befitting the foiled ambitions of his father.

Will married Azubah Jenks Culver, an Albany girl. She was an attractive woman, a self-taught musician and artist, who gave Will a veneer of culture and refinement.

Together the young couple started a family of their own. Still, I can't help but think that the echo of his grandmother's curse must have tormented Will as he watched the successive births of his children. Daughters, all daughters. Of Azubah and Will's five offspring, there was only one son, William Henry.

And what, he must have wondered, would become of the boy? And what supernatural sword must be suspended above his own throat? All he could do was work hard and pray and hope to avoid the Hayden Curse.

It is known that the Haydens turned to spiritualism in the 1850s. Though the character and content of their séances are unrecorded, it is likely Will sought the spirits' advice in business (where he was successful) and in dealing with his grandmother's malediction (at which he would fail entirely).

Although Will attained modest success as a farmer and as a cooper, his ambitions were more grandiose. With some experience as a civil engineer, he was able to try his hand at railroad building. He began with a contract in New Hampshire, constructing a line between Nashua and Quebec, Canada.

Will's timing couldn't have been better. He was so successful, he extended his work as far away as Michigan. Railroad contracts often took him out of Albany—perhaps beyond the reach of the curse. In any event, Will unquestionably prospered; he earned a fortune building more than 586 miles of rail line. By 1854 the wealth he had amassed permitted him to start building the stately Hayden mansion that still stands today.

It is commonly believed that the ostentatious residence on 1,300 acres was intended to show his neighbors just what money and ambition could do. Another layer of speculation suggests he may have been flaunting his immunity to the curse. Whatever his motive, Will was driven to build bigger, better, and more flamboyantly than anything else for miles around.

Made from brick locally kilned and granite hauled all the way from Barre, Vermont, the grand Hayden house could only be perceived as a conspicuous show of wealth, a visual testament to that American epoch when profiteering and railroad expansion were at their height.

A remarkably high-style Greek Revival building with Georgian characteristics, the three-story structure had many unique features, including, on its top floor, a full ballroom with barrel-vaulted ceiling, performing stage, and spring floor. Will also installed the area's first modern bathroom and central heating system, capable of burning 6-foot logs.

Will even employed servants—something unheard of in the Vermont north country at the time. But if maids and butlers contributed to his self-perception as a country squire, he also indulged in a kind of reverse snobbery, a false humility locally perceived as a benign eccentricity.

A century later, in a 1963 article for *Vermont Life* magazine, historian Louis Lamoureux tells a revealing story:

> [Will] favored old clothes, and when about the farm usually wore the old farmer's long blue smock, wide-brimmed hat and boots. [One] day when he was returning from a sheep pasture on foot, looking his worst . . . a passing Newport [Vermont] minister offered a lift in his buggy. Noting Will's poor apparel the minister asked to send Will a pair of his old trousers. Will allowed that he could use them. As the horse trotted up to the mansion driveway, Will told his benefactor to drive in. The minister asked if he worked there. "I own the place," Will admitted, and, it being close to dinner time, he gave orders for "the best meal you can prepare." As the dazed clergyman was driving away later, Will called after him: "Don't forget the pants."

At the same time, less comic forces seemed to be at work. From the moment Will and his family took up residence in the mansion, things started to go wrong. For the Haydens, tragedy would soon become a way of life.

First, Will's sight began to fail him. It was a gradual thing, but with its decline, his business dealings became progressively more difficult.

Townspeople began to whisper that Will—like his father, William—was secretly engaged in the dirty business of smuggling. Otherwise, how could he have become so successful? Though it was illegal for Chinese laborers to enter the United States at that time, Oriental workers kept appearing on Will's railroad jobs. He *must* have been sneaking them in from Canada, hiding them in secret rooms and tunnels in the house, then dispatching them to work in effect as slave labor.

Will and Azubah's marriage, too, was suddenly in trouble. Will and his wife had a serious falling-out over the attentions paid to her by a hired man whenever Will was away. The employee was subsequently found badly beaten. After that event, Will and Azubah were permanently estranged. Though they lived together in the Hayden Mansion, they kept separate quarters and communicated only via a third party, their son Henry, or a servant. This pattern continued until the end of their days.

## THE THIRD GENERATION

Of Will and Azubah's five children—Henry, Julia, Mary, Azubah, and Alvina—only four lived to enjoy the grand house. Those who didn't die young failed to produce male heirs. Daughter Mary took sick after giving birth to her fourth child, and went insane, remaining that way until her death in 1867.

Daughter Julia was next to go. She gave up the Hayden name when she married William Blaisdell, and she passed on without producing male heirs.

Perhaps most significant, Will's only son, Henry, began acting strangely. Though he'd often seemed a bit "unreliable," he now appeared overtly unstable. Yet even with his sanity in question, Henry married Lydia Crosby of Waterville, Maine. This union was to produce four children: three girls and one boy. Willimina died in 1894 of pneumonia. Carrie died in 1910 of tuberculosis. But the couple's son, William Andrew Hayden—who now provided the only hope of carrying on the family name—was to suffer the Hayden Curse in full view of his parents. This boy—Will Hayden's only grandson, Henry Hayden's sole male heir—died in 1871 at age five.

## THEN THERE WAS ONE

Even with his failing eyesight, Will lived to see his children die and his fortune erode in the hands of an unstable son—the last male to bear the Hayden name.

In 1883 Will suffered a final blow, when a severe stroke took away his remaining sight and subsequently ended his life. At the point of Will's death, two generations of Haydens had fallen. Now Will's unstable son, Henry, remained—the only third-generation male and the final target of Mercie Dale's curse.

No one has been able to diagnose what effects living under threat of a curse had on Henry.

And no one has been able to analyze Henry's manipulations of the family fortune. Some say he tried to save it; others say he contrived to steal what was left of it. All we know is that his unorthodox financial shenanigans so alienated his mother, Azubah, that she cut him out of her will.

Still, he kept up the appearance of prosperity by raising cows, racing horses, and quite possibly by continuing to smuggle Chinese laborers. It is certain that Henry made various efforts to pry money out of the estate—which remained confused and unsettled for many years.

Henry fell to the curse in 1910, a victim of massive cerebral hemorrhage.

Now there was only one person bearing the Hayden name left alive, Henry's daughter Aremenia Mamie Hayden. All she inherited was a bunch of bad debts and a questionable family reputation. Humiliated, unmarried, and chronically ill, the solitary spinster retreated to property owned by her mother's family in Waterville, Maine.

There, on February 20, 1927, she died poverty-stricken and alone. The last victim of Mercie Dale's curse, the last of the Haydens.

## AUTHOR'S NOTE

Though the Haydens were gone, the Hayden house seemed to struggle to maintain a life of its own. In 1913 the mansion and its contents were sold for $8,300. Apparently the money went to pay unsettled debts. The new owner sold it to some Canadians who, local legend holds, involved the place in bootlegging and alcohol smuggling. Supposedly the tunnels and secret hiding places active during the "Chinese smuggling era" were once again put to use.

The Canadians sold out in 1922 after packing up what remained of the Haydens' possessions—including a rosewood piano and other expensive furnishings—and sending them north by rail to Canada. On the way, the train derailed. One—just one—of the many freight cars separated and rolled down an embankment, where it crashed, completely destroying all contents. As if to demonstrate that Mercie was still up to her old tricks, the wrecked railroad car was the one containing the Hayden furniture.

After that the Hayden Mansion, like its namesake family, went rapidly downhill. Chunks of land were sold off, barns burned, fire took down the brick ell.

The neglected house stood empty for about forty years,

open to the elements and all variety of intruders. Curious townsfolk would sneak in at night, only to be frightened away by inexplicable noises, odd sights, and sometimes the sound of music that seemed to be coming from the upstairs ballroom.

Viewers from afar reported lights moving mysteriously through the fields surrounding the old place. Perhaps, they speculated, they were the ghosts of nameless Chinese laborers who'd passed away while hiding within the ancient walls.

And to this day some folks from Albany maintain that ghosts still walk in the house's chill, dark hallways. If some long-dead Hayden lingers there, he—or possibly she—would be the only Hayden to survive the destructive dictate of Mercie Dale's curse.

## REBIRTH

In 1957 the long-deserted house and seven surrounding acres were purchased by William and Evelyn Chadwick. For nearly half a century, the family has been carefully restoring the old house, in some cases brick by brick. They've even recovered many of the original Hayden furnishings. Though the Reverend Chadwick has passed on, Mrs. Chadwick still lives on the premises. When I visited in 2003 for a talk and a tour, Evelyn Chadwick and her grandson Chad Graham showed me around. Although the three enormous barns and connecting underground tunnels are gone, the main house looks pretty much as it did during its heyday.

They showed me old photographs of the house as it once was, including ancient images of Henry and the Widow Azubah. I also poked through Will Hayden's account books, tried to decipher his handwriting, and viewed the spot where a plasterer's signature in a closet—TITUS 1854—set the date of the house's construction. In the vaulted attic ballroom, tiny doors concealed beneath built-in benches may once have admitted smuggled Chinese workers or Prohibition-era booze to hidden compartments under the eaves. I puzzled at what appear to be fireplaces but are in reality furnace registers with grilled openings framed by mantels of cast iron and marbleized wood.

I didn't see any ghosts, though the Chadwicks told me that stories of specters persist to this day. Townspeople inclined to such talk speculate that Hayden haunts may include the original William Hayden, doing eternal penance in the spirit world. Or the wailing wraith of Will's lunatic daughter Mary, who died in the house. Or possibly her mother, Azubah, making music from the celestial realm.

But if Haydens still walk the halls, it would be inconsistent with the curse. For Mercie's malediction was designed to rid the world of Haydens forever.

## THE CHADWICK CURE

After nearly half a century the Chadwicks, like the rest of Albany, continue to refer to their home as the Hayden house. But clearly the Chadwicks' generous and restorative spirit has evicted any malevolence that might have temporarily lingered.

Though the Haydens are long gone, the house lives on. And young Chad Graham is as committed as his grandparents were to keeping it alive. Still, he says, there is a lot to be done.

It took three generations to destroy the house of Hayden. It may take three generations of Chadwicks to bring it back.

And to keep its story alive.

# FATE AND THE PHOENIX

*Her countenance once seen was not easily forgotten. Her eyes, where the fire of youth appeared to be supplied with no holy flame, sent forth their scrutiny beneath brows, arched upon a forehead of more than common character; her features were strongly marked, and a powerful intellect still illuminated them; but it was a light that only served to make more visible, the malignant passions inscribed there.*

—Theodore Sedgwick, *Hints to My Countrymen*

## NO GHOST SHIP

Vermont has what is perhaps the dubious distinction of being the only New England state without a seacoast. Consequently, we lack many tales of high adventure: the pirates, ghost ships, and nautical disasters that are so dear to the hearts of our five neighbors.

We do, however, have a great body of water: Lake Champlain. Historian Ralph Nading Hill describes it as "the most historic body of water in the western hemisphere: a silver dagger from Canada to the heartland of the American colonies that forged the destiny of France and England in America, and of the United States."

Vermont's great lake is roughly 110 miles long, 400 feet deep, and 11 miles at its widest point. It was "discovered" by Samuel de Champlain in 1609. Though it is not a sea, it nonetheless holds its share of mysterious secrets, including treasures, haunted islands, and even a sea serpent, the so-called Lake Champlain Monster.

Frankly, I have always felt a little cheated that there are no ghost ships on Lake Champlain. With all the Revolutionary War battles, 1812 skirmishes, and Prohibition-era rum-running, you'd think there would be at least one Yankee version of the Flying Dutchman cursed to drift amid the swirling fog and scattered islands until doomsday.

Alas, there is no phantom vessel. There is, however, a story containing all the dramatic elements of a ghost ship in the making. You might call it the *Titanic* of Lake Champlain water disasters: the burning of the steamboat *Phoenix*.

Mr. Hill proclaims the episode the "most dramatic on American waterways." But even he admits we have no precise and perfectly definitive explanation for what caused the conflagration. We have suspicions. We have theories. We even have a historical consensus based on the most likely scenario. But the fact is, despite all our science of historical reconstruction, we lack the time machine required to return us to that fatal night in 1819 when the *Phoenix* went down.

In short, there is no way to find out for sure what happened. Instead, we must be content with one of three principal explanations: the most widely accepted—carelessness of a crew member; the lesser known—sabotage by a rival shipping company; or the most arcane, most rarely articulated, and most readily ignored—the intervention of the supernatural: a curse.

## LUXURY LINER

In the early nineteenth century, steamboats provided the only convenient link from New York to Montreal. They were used by all classes of society—anyone one who could pay the fare.

The *Phoenix*, a 146-foot paddle wheeler, was the most plush and well appointed of its day: the height of luxury on Lake Champlain. The cost for full round-trip passage was $10, which included board and lodging.

Belowdecks, stylishly furnished gentleman's and lady's cabins provided easy access to the stateroom, a smoking room, even a barbershop. Nearby, the captain's cabin and office bordered the kitchen and pantry. Cleverly designed storage space concealed stacked cordwood to fuel the cookstoves. On deck, a canvas awning at the stern shaded passengers from the hot sun while protecting them from noxious black smoke that billowed from a smokestack at the middle of the boat. Twenty-five-foot housings covered the powerful paddle wheels. Sturdy safety railings stretched around the whole circumference of the deck.

And she was fast, too. She could chug along up the lake at a good 8 miles per hour!

Typically the *Phoenix* made its regular round trip twice a week from Whitehall, New York, to St. Johns, Quebec. Two years before it burned, the ship had transported Pres. James Monroe. The next year it relocated the remains of Gen. Richard Montgomery, who had fallen in the 1775 siege of Quebec.

At 11:00 P.M. on the fatal night of September 4, 1819, the *Phoenix* had just picked up passengers in Burlington, Vermont, and was setting off toward Canada.

Capt. Jehaziel Sherman had taken unexpectedly ill and was home with a fever, leaving his twenty-one-year-old son Richard to take command. The young man had been up all the previous night preparing for his newfound responsibilities, so he had retired, exhausted, just before midnight.

Altogether there were forty-six people aboard, passengers and crew. Among them was John Purple Howard, a Burlington hotel owner. He carried a carpetbag containing $8,000 from the Bank of Burlington to deliver to Montreal. Together, he and his son occupied a cabin near the pantry.

## THE HORROR BEGINS

At about midnight—just as the *Phoenix* passed Colchester Reef—
John Howard smelled smoke.

He got up to investigate. When he saw flames in the common area, he ran shouting through the cabins, pounding on
doors, alerting everyone.

The rest happened all too quickly.

Within moments, engine oil caught fire. Tongues of fire
leaped through the paddle-wheel housing. A brisk north wind
fanned the flames into an inferno. Now the deck was ablaze;
fire enveloped the entire center of the boat.

The canvas tarp—intended to protect passengers from
smoke and the sun's heat—ignited, smoking and blazing on its
own. Spires of flame cut John Howard off from his money,
singeing his hair and eyebrows. His son tried to reach the carpetbag by climbing over the wheelhouse, but intense heat
drove him back.

Despite the valiant efforts of young Captain Sherman,
chaos and confusion reigned. The fire quickly grew out of control; so did the passengers. People—most in their nightclothes—
screamed and pushed, fighting their way to the lifeboats.

Captain Sherman, a revolver in each hand, shouted instructions, trying to enforce order. Women climbed aboard the star-
board lifeboat as the *Phoenix*'s levelheaded stewardess, one Mrs.
Wilson, handed them their belongings. With twenty people
aboard—including John Howard's son, who had somehow managed to retrieve the precious carpetbag—the rescue vessel
reached capacity and was launched for nearby Providence
Island.

Fourteen more individuals climbed into the port lifeboat.

Although there was room for those remaining, a crew member—later identified as the engineer, MacVane—panicked, seized control, and cut the boat adrift before it was full.

Eleven people were thus abandoned on the flaming deck, among them the brave stewardess, still trying to assist and calm the terrified passengers. Of these, some jumped directly into the frigid water. One man clung to the rudder until fire burned it off. He used the severed piece to save himself.

Nonswimmers and less able travelers were stranded as the *Phoenix* burned around them. Cries for assistance from those who could not swim were pitiable. The scoundrel MacVane refused to go back. To those who insisted he turn the lifeboat around and save those stranded in the water or on deck, the engineer shouted, "I'll knock the first man overboard who should rise to make the attempt."

All this happened within the first hour of September 5. They were 14 miles from Burlington, 4 miles from Colchester Point, and 2 miles from Providence Island.

As lifeboats and swimmers made their way to Providence Island, the flaming *Phoenix* drifted toward the reef. Of the forty-six people on board, all but six made it to safety. Mrs. Wilson, the stalwart stewardess, was among the casualties.

Capt. Richard Sherman was the last to leave. The courageous young man remained aboard till the last minute, throwing things into the water—tables, benches, barrels—anything on which people could float.

He was later discovered unconscious and nearly dead on the rocks of Stave Island.

John Howard's son managed to save the moneybag, only to have it stolen while the young man continued to assist troubled survivors. Contemporary documents attest that the thief was quickly apprehended and the money recovered.

Rescue boats hurried from Burlington and nearby towns as

the towering flames that so discolored the night sky began to diminish. Finally they vanished altogether when the *Phoenix* burned to the waterline. Its skeleton sank off Colchester Reef.

## AN INVESTIGATION

Afterward, of course, there was an inquest and a great deal of discussion about just how the fire had started. Although certain circumstantial evidence suggested sabotage by a competing company, no proof of foul play could be discovered.

The theory that eventually became accepted as historical fact attributes the whole affair to a crew member's carelessness. The scenario goes like this:

Apparently the custom among crew members working all night was to pause for a midnight snack.

As the *Phoenix* beat its way down the moonlit lake, some-one—never identified—was in the pantry having a bite to eat. Presumably a candle was left burning on a shelf. In time its flame heated, then ignited, the wood of the shelf above. A few minutes later the entire galley was in flames. Fire spread to the rest of the vessel, leading to the horrific events described above.

So that's the story.

And it may be true.

That's how it was published in the newspapers, and that's what you'll read in the history books. In many ways it was the most advantageous story for all concerned (except maybe the engineer, MacVane). After all, the *Phoenix* fire might have dis-couraged prospective passengers from boarding other boats had everyone not been made to understand that its cause was something as mundane as a candle in the pantry. A tragedy to be sure, but one that could have occurred on any ship or, for that matter, in any building on land. In those days people understood and accepted fire as one of life's dangers.

But there is an alternate explanation.

## MALIGNANT PASSIONS

According to author Theodore Sedgwick in his book *Hints to My Countrymen*, published just seventeen years after the calamity, Lake Champlain's greatest nautical disaster had far darker origins: It was the direct consequence of a confrontation and a curse.

This little-known account argues that events unfolded just a bit differently.

On an earlier voyage of the *Phoenix*—just as it was boarding to leave Burlington—an old woman with a withered arm presented herself to the elder captain, Jehaziel Sherman, who normally commanded the boat.

Mr. Sedgwick writes, "[Her] age and miserable appearance would have excited no other emotion than compassion, had it not been, that from under a bonnet which imperfectly covered her disordered cap, and grisly locks, a pair of sunken, but piercing eyes, emitted a glance of such a character as to create a stronger and less amiable feeling."

With no apparent timidity she announced that she'd be traveling with him to Canada, but made no offer to pay her fare. Captain Sherman tried to be pleasant about it. "Indeed, old mother," he said jokingly, "we don't take passengers on those terms; that would be but a losing concern, you know."

When she still refused to pay, the captain turned her away at the dock. Soon the old woman was lost in the crowd. The captain, in the bustle of preparing to launch, quickly forgot about her.

Yet later, after they had cast off and were well on their way north, Captain Sherman inexplicably saw her on board.

Surprised and a bit bewildered, he investigated. When he discovered she still had not paid for her passage, he instructed one of the crewmen to take a lifeboat and put her ashore immediately.

She complied, but when the lifeboat had cast off, she faced the captain and said, "Behold how I sign your destruction! How I inscribe on the viewless air the reward of your folly!" With that she raised her withered arm and made motions in the air as if she were writing. At the same time she pronounced words in some unintelligible language. French? Or perhaps some Native American dialect? We just don't know.

But whatever she said, in time the witnesses came to understand that she had uttered a curse on the captain, his family, and his ship. And soon the mechanism of that curse would begin its evil work.

### EARLY SIGNS

Before the *Phoenix*'s next voyage north, Capt. Jehaziel Sherman took sick. Perhaps it is important to note that it was the fires of fever that kept him home in bed while his son Richard, unmindful of the disaster ahead, took over as captain.

With the younger Captain Sherman in command, the cursed *Phoenix*—at midnight, and at roughly the same spot the old woman had been put ashore—mysteriously burst into flames. Though surrounded by water, there was no way to extinguish the fire as the paddle wheeler burned and sank in the cold waves of Colchester Reef.

Could the mysterious old woman's malignant will have

sickened Capt. Jehaziel Sherman, brought down his boat, and nearly caused the death of his son?

According to Theodore Sedgwick, Lake Chaplain's greatest nautical disaster was most decidedly the consequence of a curse.

## AUTHOR'S NOTE

We must each decide for ourselves, as no clue survives in the underwater wreckage.

The *Phoenix* remained hidden for nearly 160 years, until—on August 21, 1978—it was unexpectedly discovered by scuba divers Don Mayland, Dick Hubbard, and John Mudgett.

Its reappearance acted as catalyst for the formation in 1980 of the Champlain Maritime Society, an organization of underwater archaeologists, historians, divers, and laypeople dedicated to preserving and documenting the lake's heritage. The Phoenix Project became the group's first major study. In 1986 the society was incorporated as the Lake Champlain Maritime Museum, where exhibits pertaining to the *Phoenix* may be viewed.

So, like its namesake the mythological bird, the steamship *Phoenix* succumbed to flames and sank until, after more than a century, it has in a sense been reborn. Today it lies in 60 to 110 feet of water and is one of several exhibits divers can visit in the state of Vermont's underwater preserves.

There the inscrutable artifact holds its secrets, natural and perhaps supernatural.

# THE WITCH AND THE VIRGIN

*Yet these active folks had leisure for a superstitious fear,*
*And they told all sorts of stories of the evils hovering near.*

–Sybil Ramsey, "The Deserted Village"

## THE WITCH

I had an unsettling sense of déjà vu the moment I drove into Pepperell, Massachusetts.

Sweating, muscles tense, too tightly gripping the wheel, I felt as if I were about to drive straight into a remake of *The Blair Witch Project*.

What I mean is, I was preparing to venture into a ghost town, a town that history tells us had been devastated by a witch's curse. A town where people had vanished and died without explanation, and one that–to this very day–carries an odd, uncomfortable stigma along with its aura of mystery and malevolence.

"It's awful quiet up there," a librarian in town told me, somewhat noncommittally, as I asked directions to the abandoned village.

Though the ghost town is still referred to as North Pepperell, most modern maps have dropped the designation entirely, somehow completing the destruction of what once had been a thriving New England community–the earliest part of Pepperell to be settled and devoted to commerce.

The area I sought is roughly defined by the Nissitissit River on the west, the beginning of Prescott Street at the southern tip, and Hollis Street on the east. The New Hampshire border makes up the northern perimeter of the former town.

"Is there anything still there?" I asked the librarian.

"The school's still standing," she said. "And Colonel Prescott's place."

Col. William Prescott, locally famed for shouting, "Don't fire till you see the whites of their eyes," at the battle of Bunker Hill, built his rambling mansion in 1749. Somehow, it survived the horror.

"But the ruins, are any still visible?"

"Oh, yes. Some of them. There's an old mill. You can see its foundation. And if you walk along the river you can see cellar holes. You can see where the railroad used to run. . . ." She paused, looking contemplative. "I'm not really sure what else is up there," she said. "I really never go there."

But she was painting a picture of utter devastation. And I was having second thoughts about making the trip, just a straight, short shot north from the library.

## LINGERING EVIL

Among those who know the story, there is a good deal of speculation about when the witch's curse ended—or if it has ended at all.

Certainly the once populated town has never been densely resettled. Could that be the direct result of the curse? Or is it simply a fear the evil may still be in effect?

Some speculate that the last act of preternatural assault occurred as recently as 1920, when Miss Florence Sibley was found dead in her gloomy old home. The elderly woman, uncared for and alone, had died of starvation. Her ruined corpse wasn't discovered for more than a week after she left this world.

What had she done to deserve such a sad fate?

Nothing, perhaps. But then again, it was she who first assembled the "facts" of the witch's tale, formalized them, wrote them up, and made them public at a DAR meeting at the Prudence Wright Chapter House in 1914. In effect, Florence Sibley brought the North Pepperell Witch out of the closet and reintroduced her to the townspeople.

It is her history upon which all other histories seem to be built.

## ON THE SCENE

Standing on Prescott Street, north of the river and not far from the brick schoolhouse on my right, I contemplate a row of sturdy rock maples. They're gigantic. Their girth and huge gargoyle-like burls suggest they have stood there a long, long time. Perhaps those trees are the only surviving witnesses to the tragedy.

Before stepping from the safety of the dirt shoulder through the gateway formed by those ancient trunks, before setting off alone into the lightless woodland, I try to analyze what is making me feel so hesitant, so shaky.

Is it because it is so dark in there?

At the library the sun was blasting and everyone was complaining about the heat. Here, everything is in shadows. The air is noticeably cooler. A ubiquitous stillness is oddly conspicuous. In all the time I've been standing here, not a single car has passed.

Darkness, possibly. But more likely, I conclude, it's timing.

Most of the curse stories I have studied are distorted or

dimmed by historical shadow. In many instances a curse's artic-
ulation and its aftermath occurred in early colonial times—the
mid-1600s—and were more often than not the work of an
Indian shaman. Witches—and their curses—are most frequently
associated with the witchcraft craze of 1692 Salem.

But what happened in North Pepperell was far more recent.
Too recent. The beginning of the nineteenth century. Some
chroniclers place its commencement date at 1820.

What could this woman have done to convince enlight-
ened nineteenth-century Americans that she was a witch?

And once accused, what had she done in return?

## LOCAL HISTORY

In the early 1800s North Pepperell was a prosperous and flourishing little place. The town history describes it as "a Puritan
town," so we may presume its citizens were hardworking and
pious people.

The population was large enough to support a gristmill, a
sawmill, a carding and clothier mill, a hay rake business, a
blacksmith, a cigar manufacturer, a tavern and boardinghouse,
a store, a post office, a school, even the inevitable casket maker.

Numerous homesteads lined the roads and river, and dap-
pled the well-tended fields. The farms were said to be as fine
and productive as any in the entire country.

We get the picture of an ideal little village where everyone
was happy and industrious, where the children were sensible
and well mannered, and where the entire community
embraced the notion of strong neighborly values.

Then—for some reason—a cloud darkened the horizon.

Sometime after the War of 1812, an eccentric old woman

arrived in town. Some sources say her surname was Lovejoy. Apparently she was a stranger to everyone as she went about the solitary business of moving into an abandoned cabin on the bank of the Nissitissit River not far from the schoolhouse. She did little to improve the place and less to mingle with her neighbors.

Nonetheless, she managed to get in trouble with some of them. She kept a few cows, pigs, and chickens, but she let them all run loose. They annoyed the neighbors and frightened their children.

Needless to say, her presence and odd practices inspired a lot of talk.

People remarked on her odd mode of dress, including the handkerchief she wore on her head. The less charitable made comments about her unappealing physical attributes; she was stooped and walked funny. No one asked her where she had come from, and apparently she never volunteered the information.

One day she wasn't there. The next day she was.

And suddenly everything changed.

## A WITCH IN THEIR MIDST

Local history books never clearly state what she did to make the good people of North Pepperell elevate her stature from neighborhood nuisance to full-fledged witch. In a 1971 *Yankee Magazine* article, Pepperell resident Mabel Willard simply says, "Her queer looks, dress, and actions proclaimed her a witch to the townspeople."

Pretty flimsy evidence. More flimsy than the "spectral evidence" at Salem.

I can't help but hope there was more involved to incite the next sequence of events. Around 1820 some of the local men, no doubt prodded by the local women, decided to take action. Three of them abducted her. Two restrained her while the third took a red-hot branding iron from the fire and applied it to the center of her forehead.

For some days she languished, retreating from the indignity. Soon after, she left town. But before leaving, she uttered words that reverberated long after she'd vanished.

She laid a curse on the men and on the village, swearing that the river would dry up and run away. The mills and houses would be consumed by fire. The inhabitants would flee from the village as from a pestilence. That in a few decades no one would be living where once was a thriving community, and that even the farms just outside the village would not escape her wrath. "In every home," she said, "the 'death angel' will make his entry in an unusual manner."

Then she disappeared into the wilderness surrounding their little island of civilization.

## A TRAIL OF TRAGEDY

After the curse, nothing was the same in the village of North Pepperell. The songs of the children quieted. Good cheer among neighbors turned to averted eyes and somber silence.

Tragedy after tragedy struck the little border town. Fire annihilated the sawmill and gristmill, as if something malignant and powerful were striking at the source of their building materials and food supply.

Putnam Shattuck's shoe factory was also lost to the hellish flames. More mills burned: a cotton batting and shoddy mill, two paper mills, and a cloth processing business.

New mills were built or rebuilt, but each fell to the ravenous flames. It was as if every source of livelihood—except that of the coffin maker—was being shut down.

Some people fled to find work elsewhere, "as from a pestilence."

Soon the houses, one by one, became tenantless. The dam that had so long supplied the water power for the village burst, and the river—just as the witch had said—lost depth and "ran away."

Several articles recounting the curse describe how almost every house was touched by tragedy. Suicide claimed unprecedented numbers of victims; on one street the occupants of three houses died by their own hand.

But far stranger deaths made people pause and shudder in horror, silently contemplating who might be next or openly discussing how the "death angel" would make his next entry in an "unusual manner."

A farmer inexplicably fell over in his chair, an incident that might have been almost comic had he not broken his neck and died on the spot.

An elderly man choked on a piece of meat and died breathless, blue, and terrified before the eyes of his helpless family.

Another man was killed when he fell from his wagon after his horse bolted for reasons that were never discerned.

A farmer was murdered in his home—or more precisely he died there under suspicious circumstances—though no motive or perpetrator was ever discovered.

A four-year-old boy playing by the river fell in and drowned. He had been named after his father and grandfather. The family name ended with him.

Perhaps most mysterious of all, a young woman who went out to the barn one morning to get some milk disappeared. Somewhere on that short walk, she vanished completely. It was as if she had stepped off the face of the earth.

As the few remaining businesses folded for lack of patrons, people continued to move away. Those who remained lived in a heightened state of nervousness, never knowing when tragedy would strike down another of them. Tense, fearful, and stressed beyond history's ability to reconstruct, marital problems reached epic numbers. Children grew surly, cruel, and unmanageable.

In time North Pepperell became a deserted village. Yet even without occupants, untenanted houses continued to burn or fall down under the cold weight of repeated winter storms.

Some believe the last victims of the curse fell in the early 1900s. Two elderly sisters living on the perimeter of the village saw a fire in the woods behind their house. There was no way to summon help, so they tried to put it out on their own. One became trapped; her body was discovered later . The other vanished without a trace. Then, little by little, the forest began to reclaim what had once been its own. And that's what I saw when I stepped between the ancient maples and into the woods of North Pepperell. A "deserted village" in name only, for there was no village at all.

Cellar holes could easily be mistaken for fieldstones. What was left of a mill was a rock wall visibly hugging the dark, slow moving waters of the Nissitissit. Everything else was gone forever or shrouded with vines, trees, brush, and a blanket of dead leaves.

## NOTHING ADDS UP

Yet susceptible as I was to sensing the presence of evil or the supernatural, other thoughts intruded as I walked along the old railroad bed. Some kind of bird—a blue jay, I think—squawked angrily from the treetops as if warning me away.

Yes, I could see the wreckage of a town, but only in my imagination. Something had happened here—but the details just didn't add up. What had Mistress Lovejoy done to bring down the wrath of the townspeople?

Why had they branded her? Neither history nor folklore mentions witches being branded. In fact, I could not think of another instance where this had happened. It was simply not consistent with either fact or superstition.

If any unseen eyes were watching me, it might have looked as if I fled to avoid a preternatural confrontation. But the fact is, I thought my time would be more productively spent at the library, not in the woods.

## SAFE AMONG THE STACKS

Reference librarian Nancy Hayes Clune gave me a collection of material relevant to the North Pepperell Witch. Among the clippings, I found a fascinating pair of 1987 newspaper articles by Debbie Song.

Ms. Song has done some impressive analytical research to cast new light on this dark tale. Her theory, in essence, is that the whole witch tale may have been concocted by the citizens of Pepperell to cover up a dastardly deed of their own.

Perhaps encoded in the texts of primary Pepperell Witch chroniclers Florence Sibley and Mabel Willard, the discerning eye can detect the truth about what really happened. You might say the "witch" may be the skeleton in Pepperell's collective closet.

Much of Debbie Song's speculation has to do with the identity of the so-called witch, the mysterious Mistress Lovejoy.

Florence Sibley and Mabel Willard both say North Pepperell

was the first and primary business section of town. Yet historical records show there was no church there.

Why not? Its absence is especially noteworthy in light of a popular town history's (*The Pepperell Reader*) proclamation that Pepperell was a Puritan town.

Perhaps North Pepperell was not as large as the witch tales suggest. It was large enough to have a school, but too small for a church. Perhaps we should be concerned with the whole of Pepperell, not just the so-called north village.

Also, as previously stated, neither history nor folklore mentions branding as a mode of dealing with witches. It wasn't practiced before or during that most maniacal of witch scares, the 1692 Salem debacle. But there was another population that the Puritans felt perfectly justified in branding: heretics. And in early New England, those heretics were more often than not Quakers.

Other than the accused witches themselves, and possibly the Indians, no population suffered greater brutality at the hands of the Puritans than did the Quakers.

Notice that the tale begins right after the War of 1812—a war the peace-loving Quakers overtly opposed. If Mistress Lovejoy had been an outspoken Quaker, she would have been at political odds with many of her neighbors. Also, many Quaker women considered it a mission to remind the pious Puritans that they were most emphatically *not* God's chosen people. Any dialogue of that nature would have focused additional scorn on poor Mistress Lovejoy.

And Quakers did not attend church. As a "society of Friends," they attended meetings at meetinghouses. Oddly, what people have come to call "the school" in North Pepperell is, upon closer examination, an example of Quaker architecture. A meetinghouse, perhaps? "The steeple-like appendage," Ms. Song tells us, "added to the building in 1833 resembles other Quaker Meeting Houses."

Further, she says, "An examination of the cemetery in Pepperell shows many gravestones marked with Quaker eulogies."

But still there is the persistence of *The Pepperell Reader* proclaiming that the town was Puritan!

Well, in reality there were two populations in town, Puritans and Quakers. And some of the former, mentioned in Miss Sibley's and Ms. Willard's texts, were powerful and influential individuals.

North Pepperell's "witch" was most probably a Quaker woman, and quite possibly a zealot. Apparently outspoken, unusually dressed, even—according to Florence Sibley—to the point of wearing a handkerchief on her head, a Quaker custom.

It was not uncommon to call a Quaker woman a witch. But it was meant more as an insult than an accusation, on the order of calling her a heretic.

If Quakers and Puritans shared the town, then the town was split. Ill feelings were the predictable result. There were political divisions, philosophical splits, and, perhaps most provocative of all, the inevitable commingling of groups and individuals—eventually even marriages.

Debbie Song concludes that a woman was indeed branded in Pepperell. That she was a Quaker, not a witch. And that her assailants were Misters Farrar, Prescott, and Wolcott, the only men mentioned by the historians.

If true, we may be certain there never was a curse. Quakers didn't curse people or villages. They did, however, make predictions; their publications are full of them.

It is likely that after suffering the indignities inflicted upon her by her trio of assailants, Mistress Lovejoy made a few predictions of her own. Some of these forecasts—as with those made by any insightful individual—seem to have come true:

After the dam burst the river dried up, though not completely.

Many of the mills and houses were consumed by fire.

The inhabitants did flee from the pestilence of economic decline.

In a few decades, infighting, disaster, and decline caused most people to relocate from the north village.

And of course the "death angel" touched many homes, as it eventually does in every home.

## FINAL QUESTIONS

So it seems quite likely that the Puritans of Pepperell did burn someone with a branding iron: a Quaker, not a witch. But somehow—at least in the folk memory of the townspeople—the self-protective fiction of a witch branding seems far less egregious. More palatable. Maybe, at this point, even colorful.

But witch or Quaker, the Pepperell story leads to one important consideration as we study curse stories in general. How can we tell the difference between a curse and a prediction?

And how often do we confuse one with the other?

## AUTHOR'S NOTE

It seems highly coincidental to me, if not downright odd, that the appearance of one mystery woman in Pepperell should be followed, almost two centuries later, by the arrival of another.

I often think of this sort of dual phenomenon as "the balance of supernature": If something disproportionately evil occurs, it is likely that something of extraordinary good will be close on its heels . . . or at least something equally vexing.

So the footnote to the Pepperell Witch story is this:

A resident of Heald Street, Noel Dube, was visited by the Virgin Mary. Why she picked Pepperell, or Mr. Dube, is a mystery beyond the scope of this book. Apparently—in typical Virgin Mary fashion—she instructed him to build her a shrine.

Like the rest of us, Noel Dube was unaccustomed to divine visitations. Though he was eager to comply with her request, he didn't know exactly how to go about it.

Since World War II injuries had left him in a wheelchair, Mr. Dube knew he couldn't construct the shrine himself. And, not being wealthy, he owned only one place on which to erect it: the front yard of his Heald Street home.

Undaunted, the elderly man used his meager savings to commission an artist and put him to work painting giant religious pictures, which he erected all around his yard.

In 1991 vibrantly colored scenes began to appear. A 22-by-60-foot mural depicts the holy visions experienced in Fatima, Portugal, in 1917. You can see the sun—or possibly a flying saucer—streaking across an ultrablue sky.

There's a 30-by-12-foot, gold-framed painting of Jesus. And there are fourteen oversized stations of the cross, all of which, to certain sensibilities, might be considered a bit . . . gory.

Despite all this well-intended reverence—and perhaps in some ways reminiscent of the witch's tale—Noel Dube found himself entangled in something of a religious skirmish, pitting religious freedom against property rights.

In 1999 his nearest neighbor, Phyllis Symonds, placed her nineteenth-century Colonial-style house on the market. When it didn't sell quick enough to suit her, she concluded Mr. Dube's illuminated icons and pious crowds were scaring prospective buyers away.

She argued, via a lawyer, that the pictures were billboards and therefore illegal under local rules that limit the size of signs.

Mr. Dube—taking his instructions from a higher authority—maintained that they were not signs; they were religious paintings. And under Massachusetts General Law, land that is used for religious purposes is exempt from all zoning ordinances and bylaws.

One might conclude from these two stories that Pepperell has always been rife for religious discord. But in the end another miracle apparently occurred. Phyllis Symonds sold her property.

And, as I stood at the hedgerow entrance to Mr. Dube's property in 2003 looking at the bright pictures, the newly painted house, and well-kept grounds, it appears that peace has been restored to Our Lady of Fatima Community Shrine.

And, perhaps, to Pepperell as well.

# THE TREE OF KNOWLEDGE

*See that thou marks't the spot*
*See that I'm not forgot,*
*Else cursed shall be thy lot.*

–Wendell B. Phillips, "Tree of Knowledge"

## AVOIDING DOOM

For more than 200 years, the citizens of Duxbury, Massachusetts, have been living under the threat of a curse. Taking constant preventive measures to protect themselves, they have–at least for a time–reached an uneasy truce with a vigilant nature spirit. If these measures were not undertaken, no one knows what kind of devastation may result, but most agree it would be of biblical proportions.

This town of 15,000 people, incorporated in 1637, sits on the coast of Cape Cod Bay, so potential dangers might include pestilence, fire, earthquakes, hurricanes, tidal waves, and, ultimately, dropping off into the sea.

But how real is the menace?

As local historian Dr. Reuben Peterson wrote during the Duxbury Tercentenary in 1937, "While the members of the Tercentenary Committee can not be said to be superstitious, it is just as well to be on the safe side."

~

## A VENERABLE CITIZEN

The history of this precarious situation began long before the Pilgrims landed at nearby Plymouth Rock. The initiating event was so colorless as to be unnoticed by wildlife or Native Americans: a single tiny acorn tumbled from a branch, struck the ground, bounced, settled, eventually germinated, and finally began to develop into an oak tree. As its roots burrowed into the rich primeval soil, its trunk and branches stretched toward the New England sky. By 1620 it towered above its neighbors as it watched the *Mayflower* release its eager cargo of European immigrants.

In the years to come, the oak grew old as it watched a new civilization mature around it.

The Plymouth Colony flourished to the south, while, 35 miles north, the Massachusetts Bay Colony and the city of Boston expanded. As chance would have it, the most direct connection between the two settlements ran right beside the majestic oak. Travelers along the Bay Path (today's Route 53) often stopped to rest in the shade of the old tree's branches.

At the same time, the population of Duxbury Village was growing along the coast. Eventually some twenty shipyards provided employment for families in the area. About 4 miles inland, tar pits were established not far from the venerable oak. This dark, viscous by-product of charcoal was used as caulking to seal the seams of the wooden vessels.

Tar workers clustered near their employment, founding a new settlement within Duxbury: the village of Tarkiln.

The old oak saw all this happen and—in its unique way—
soon became one of Tarkiln's most important citizens.

## GOING POSTAL

In the days of Miles Standish, there was no mail service.
Independent runners were hired to convey occasional mes-
sages or parcels between Boston and Plymouth along the Bay
Path.

This main route was intersected in Tarkiln by the road to
Duxbury, just at the corner where the old tree stood.

Of course Duxbury had no postal service of its own. As a
courtesy, the runners between the Massachusetts Bay Colony
and Plymouth used to leave or pick up messages and whatnot
for Duxbury folk at the base of the old tree. Then any passing
Duxbury citizen who discovered the packets would collect
them and deliver them to their intended recipients. Many people believe this was the first American rural free delivery
service.

In time, the amount of traffic grew along the Boston–
Plymouth route. In 1775 the Continental Congress appointed a
committee to set up a postal service independent of the British.
Benjamin Franklin was in charge. In May the Provincial
Congress established the first post office in Plymouth.

In June service was improved between Boston and
Plymouth when postal runners took to horseback. But the tradition was firmly in place: They always stopped at the foot of
the oak to drop off or pick up letters and packages.

At this point the citizens of Duxbury formalized their participation by nailing a box to the old tree—perhaps America's first postal box. It remained unlocked and unguarded until some resident, venturing out from the village, would retrieve or deliver the mail.

In 1796 the Bay Path became a stage route, with three trips a week between Boston and Plymouth. Yet the cooperative custom continued, using the old oak as a drop-off spot.

Because of its distinct role in colonial communications, the old oak became known far and wide as the Tree of Knowledge, for, in this pre-newspaper age, it was the sole point from which all Duxbury's information was gathered and dispensed. And North Bend—the intersection of the Plymouth–Boston road where the tree grew—came to be called Tree of Knowledge Corner.

So in a sense this grand old tree played an important, if passive, role in the communications system of the village and in establishing the fledgling postal service in the New World.

Alas, things changed. Sometime between the advent of the stagecoach and the coming of the Old Colony Railroad in 1845, the box on the old tree fell into disuse except in the romantic affairs of the residents. Sweethearts would slip secret notes or plans for clandestine rendezvous into its opening at night. But other than the occasional billet-doux, the old tree's prominence in the community was a thing of the past. It was relegated to the status of outsider. The area around it was neglected; the disused box secured to its trunk began to weather and decompose.

## AN EVIL WIND

Then one night a terrific storm rolled in from the sea. Heavy, mucus-colored clouds obliterated the heavens. Great trees swayed and houses trembled. Incessant lightning torched the sky, briefly transforming night into brilliant day. The roar of thunder was like the discharge of a thousand cannon.

It was as if nature were at war with Duxbury.

Within their homes, cowering inhabitants quivered while hail bombarded their rooftops. Then, just as the clock struck midnight, a dazzling flash and deafening crash jolted the entire village, sending the terrified citizens to their beds, where they trembled until morning.

Those venturing out the next day discovered that the Tree of Knowledge had not survived the storm. There it was, prostrate beside the road, its thick trunk severed and splintered by a lightning bolt. And there it stayed, left to rot in the elements—forgotten and uncared for.

Before the townspeople could finish making repairs and clearing away the rubble left by the storm, the whole village was thrown into a second uproar. An elderly patriarch from Tarkiln confessed to a group of local dignitaries that he had experienced a disturbing visitation. In a vivid dream the spirit of the venerable old oak tree appeared, chiding him and everyone in town for failing to properly recognize the familial role it had played in the success of the community. The bitter tree lamented that they hadn't even grieved its passing, when, in former days, it had been so vital to their lives, bringing everyone so much joy and even sorrow.

It was then that the grim specter issued the curse: If the spot where the oak had stood remained unmarked, that spot would be forever cursed. Plague and other dreadful events would befall the population—events far worse than the storm that had felled the tree.

Trembling like a branch in a windstorm, the old man told his story. He also confessed that he had agreed to all the spirit's demands. Considering what they had to lose, the other town fathers affirmed that the old man had done the right thing. Straightaway they abandoned their chores and went about designing a commemorative plaque. Together they made a wooden sign and put it up, like a grave marker, at the site where the tree had stood.

## AUTHOR'S NOTE

Exactly when this dramatic series of events actually occurred is a matter of speculation. In 1923 selectman Wendell B. Phillips reported that his grandfather Augustus Phillips, as a small boy, remembered seeing a sign on that spot as early as 1818. So we might guess that the curse was uttered sometime around the turn of the nineteenth century.

Since that day, whenever it was, villagers have feared the Curse of the Tree of Knowledge. The site where the grand tree stood has been continually marked. And as long as the marker stands, tradition holds that Duxbury will stave off any preternatural retribution.

According to *Boston Herald* reporter Lowell Ames Norris, "There was much public fretting" in 1923 when the sign had to come down briefly for road repairs.

But Harry Randall, who served as custodian of the sign, made sure it went right up again. "Folks in these parts think a lot of that sign," he said. "That spot has been marked longer than anybody can remember."

For a while signs succeeded signs. Harry Randall recalled three precursors that were replaced during his father's stewardship. And Harry himself remembered three subsequent signs during his own tenure. One was painted by a Mrs. Knapp of Plymouth; the next by Grace Waterman of Kingston. The last and most elaborate, painted by Fanny Burns Clark of South Duxbury, depicted a colonial stagecoach halted before the Tree of Knowledge, on which was prominently displayed what locals believed was the first rural delivery box in America.

In 1937, in honor of the Duxbury Tercentenary (and taking no chances), the painting was replaced with the sturdy granite monument that stands there today.

It reads:

TREE OF KNOWLEDGE
1774–1845
MAILBOX
ON OAK TREE
FOR
POST RIDERS
AND STAGES
BETWEEN
PLYMOUTH
AND BOSTON

It is there for all to see at Tree of Knowledge Corner, a small triangular park at the Summer and South Street intersection. Maintained by the Duxbury Rural and Historical Society, this granite barrier against supernatural assault should eternally protect Duxbury citizens from misfortune and disaster.

As selectman Phillips said at the time it was installed, "Duxbury residents of the Tarkiln District have taken effective measures to avert the curse."

# AN IDOL
# REVENGE

*Although Charles Hill's descendents left Maine, they had
apparently left one thing behind—the Chinese curse.*

–Thomas A. Verde, *Maine Ghosts and Legends*

## OUT-OF-PLACE ODDITY

In the lovely town of Naples, Maine, at the southern tip of
Long Lake, right on the village green, there's a typically New
England Methodist church with white clapboard sides and a
steeple pointing toward heaven. Behind it, in what looks like a
garage or carriage house, you'll find the Naples Historical
Society Museum.

The modest quarters couldn't be more inconspicuous.
Anyone looking for drama would drive on by without giving
the place a second thought. But that would be a mistake. For
beyond the museum's swinging doors, you'll discover one of the
most incongruous curiosities in all New England.

In the museum's dim interior, lurking among the classic car-
riages and antique medical equipment, a mysterious visage
peers at you from a shadowy corner.

Look again. Note the benignly clasped hands and the
quizzically unsettling smile on its gold enamel lips.

It's exactly what you think it is: a larger-than-life Chinese
statue. Standing an impressive 7 feet tall, it is fabricated from
wood, gold leaf, and plaster. And this is no reproduction. It's

genuine, ancient, and probably very valuable. Yet it rests here undisturbed year after year in this barely secure rural repository.

Two questions hammer at the imaginative twenty-first-century mind: How did such a thing get here? And, perhaps more important: Why doesn't anyone steal it?

The response to the former question will no doubt answer the latter.

## A CHINESE ADVENTURE

The story of Naples's out-of-place idol is no ho-hum historical yawner; it's a colorful saga of high adventure, stolen treasure, and Oriental occultism—and a sort of Down East version of King Tut's Curse.

The action begins in the late nineteenth century with Charles and Ruben Hill, two local brothers with a wanderlust and an entrepreneurial spirit. They left their home in Maine in search of wealth and adventure.

The brothers became shipowners and merchants engaged in the China tea trade.

Charles was a ship's captain. In time he was able to acquire a home and vast holdings in Tientsin, just south of Peking, China. It is certain he was involved in Chinese railroad building. Quite possibly he was a player in the opium trade that inspired escalating Chinese resentment toward foreign businesses.

Remember that China's long-maintained policy of isolation wasn't relaxed until 1834. After the economic floodgates were opened, myriad aggressive Western capitalists crashed through like a tidal wave.

The Chinese people viewed them as little more than bar-

barians, calling them *fan kuei*, or "foreign devils." No doubt Charles and Ruben—who had a reputation for bold and occasionally outrageous behavior—conformed to this diabolic description.

Between 1898 and 1900 China's anti-foreign fervor culminated in the so-called Boxer Rebellion, a final desperate effort to resist foreign influence. The dowager empress Tz'u-hsi wanted to expel all foreigners. She sanctioned militant action from the I Ho Ch'uan Society: the Society for Righteous, Harmonious Fists (in English, "Boxers").

Before the Hills—along with thousands of other foreign devils—were expelled, the brothers took care of some last-minute business.

At the coastal Tientsin Province, Charles had been eyeing a Buddhist temple known to contain gold, jewels, and other riches. Amid the violence and confusion of the Boxer uprising, the brothers entered the temple. With American-made firearms, they held the peaceful monks at bay as they went about looting the place.

With the assistance of armed employees, the Hill brothers seized three impressive golden idols.

Strangely, the monks put up little resistance as their ornate icons were carried away. One elderly monk, who seemed to be a leader, addressed Charles in a powerful voice. Though the words had no meaning to American ears, fear began to spread upon the Oriental faces.

"It is best you leave the statues," a hired hand advised the American brothers. But they paid no attention as their gazes searched the temple for more prizes.

Soon the Chinese idols, along with other pilfered property, were packed and stowed aboard their ship. And Charles and Ruben Hill successfully escaped China, heading home to Naples, Maine.

## A FEW SURPRISES

Upon unpacking their precious cargo, the Hill brothers were disappointed to discover that the idols were not made of solid gold, as they had believed.

For a moment Charles cursed his luck, but as he thought about it, he was puzzled. If they were not made of gold, why were they so heavy?

Upon more careful investigation, Charles was delighted to find that the largest statue concealed a secret compartment. Inside, the Chinese monks had stashed a sizable cache of gold coins and precious jewels. Charles was able to sell them for $300,000, a tidy sum in those days, equal to more than $6 million in today's currency.

Charles used the money to raze the family home, build a grand carriage house, and erect a stately, sixteen-room, three-story mansion overlooking Long Lake. He named it Belvue Terrace.

Five entrances all led to the grand main hall. Conspicuously at its center he proudly displayed the now empty statue, a curious 7-foot grotesquery intricately detailed with ten tiny Pekingese dogs decorating a body protected by armor and a helmet. Experts who have examined the statue suggest it depicts some sort of alms giver or—perhaps more important to our story—guardian.

But it wasn't the Hills' mansion the idol was designed to protect.

And, despite the pilfered jewels in its belly, it bore no alms for the thieving brothers.

## OTHERWORLDLY INFLUENCE

In fact, from the very first, the statue caused guests in the mansion to feel uncomfortable. Instead of admiring it, they avoided it—yet no one could say exactly why. At that point the brothers had no way of knowing the evil they had perpetrated at the Buddhist temple was subtly starting to reflect back at them.

Before they had much of a chance to enjoy their newfound wealth, grand Victorian surroundings, and *belles vues*, their good fortune began to shift. A supernatural revenge was beginning to take its course.

In the early years of the twentieth century, Charles found that his money was running low. Not knowing what else to do, he chanced a return trip to China. The Boxer uprising was over so—with luck—he could discover another opportunity for effortless fortune.

But instead he took sick with a mysterious and untreatable illness. Charles Hill died wasting away on his trip back to the United States.

At about the same time, Ruben met his end in an automobile accident. Everyone believed there was something suspiciously synchronous about the brothers' deaths.

And this was only the beginning.

Maine historian Lloyd Ferriss observes, "[A]s tragedy after tragedy struck tenants of the place . . . townspeople became convinced that priests of the pilfered temple had placed a curse on the brothers and everyone else who would live in the mansion."

Fearful there was some truth to this "curse" business, the Hills' heirs removed the statue and donated it to the Boston Museum of Fine Arts. They also removed themselves from Maine after throwing the two smaller idols into Long Lake, where they apparently still lie.

These cautious measures, however, ended nothing. When the house was sold, preternatural events continued.

## VICTIMS, ALL

John White, a legislator and retired lawyer, bought Belvue Terrace and lived there with his wife and their son, Charles. John seems to have escaped the curse, but maybe there was something about that name *Charles*.

The younger Mr. White was a published writer, a poet, and a Medal of Honor winner. In 1931 his dead body was discovered in the waters off Portland's Eastern Promenade, a revolver found "near the body and withdrawn but slightly from the holster."

Two bullets had been fired. One had struck Charles White in the heart.

Though the medical examiner ruled Charles's death a suicide, it does seem odd that the weapon was still in its holster and that two shots had been fired. Are we to presume he missed the first time, finished the job with a second shot, then reholstered his weapon?

Again—and not surprisingly—people began talking about the "curse" on the Hill property. And then another Charles entered the picture.

Charles Soden and his wife purchased Belvue in 1934 and renamed it The Hayloft.

During the summer Mrs. Soden ran it as a restaurant, tearoom, and antiques store. Her inventory was close at hand; the mansion came equipped like a veritable warehouse, filled with canopy beds and other impressive antiques. Given Naples's annual flow of summer tourists, the business had every reason to prosper.

But something was just a little out of alignment.

In 1936 Charles Soden hanged himself. Within a year his widow died suddenly and unexpectedly.

Eventually the property was purchased by a Connecticut couple, Philip and Dorothy Clark. Evidently they bought it sight unseen, through a real estate agent.

When they finally took up full-time residence in 1950, we can be sure they soon began to pick up on the place's "reputation."

To get off on the right foot, and perhaps in an effort to neutralize any lingering supernatural forces, they attempted another name change, calling the property Serenity Hill.

But their tenure was to be anything but serene. In February, four months after moving in, Dorothy took a bad fall, broke her hip, and had to be rushed to the hospital, where she remained for many months. Philip stayed alone at the mansion. Something happened during a cold, stormy night while Dorothy was away. With her husband alone in the house, Serenity Hill burned to the ground.

Townsfolk think it odd that Philip Clark died in that fire. His body, inexplicably, was discovered in the basement.

The double loss proved too much for Dorothy. Nerves and reason suddenly shattered, she was relocated to a mental hospital, where she died shortly thereafter.

## PROCEED WITH CAUTION

You might expect that the cleansing effect of the flames would have ended the curse once and for all.

But the carriage house was left standing.

It, and the land, were passed along to Dorothy Clark's

family. Some of her relatives moved to Naples and turned the carriage house into a nightclub that quickly acquired a reputation as a violent and unsavory place. Police were summoned frequently, and its infamy spread.

Locals still called it Serenity Hill, but now with a bit of Yankee irony in their voices. Some said the place was born in chaos and was sure to end that way.

When the nightclub closed, many people hoped the curse had run its course. They became more convinced of its passing when, in the late 1970s, the Living Waters Fellowship Congregation purchased the property. Surely the congregation's sanctified and spiritual presence would kill off any residual evil.

The pastor put his mobile home on the old foundation and held prayer meetings in the only original building left: the carriage house.

For a while all Naples breathed a big sigh of relief: The balance of supernature seemed to have corrected itself.

That is, until the pastor ran off with congregation's funds, the membership disbanded, and the church folded.

In 1998 the place was reborn as a mini golf course and restaurant, but—soon after—the manager's son came down with a mysterious, undiagnosable disease and, despite all medical intervention, quickly perished.

Needless to say, the family experienced hard times after that lamentable blow. Eventually, in 2002, they lost their property in what—all things considered—might have been a stroke of good luck.

The bank foreclosed, and everything was sold at auction.

That's when two brothers from Massachusetts acquired the place.

As I write this, the brothers have founded the Naples Self Storage Company on the property. One of them is living there full time.

And once again the people of Naples are holding their collective breath. As a town official told me, "You know, it's funny: Something bad has happened to everyone who's moved in up there. Every single one."

So once again, the clock is ticking . . .

## AUTHOR'S NOTE

We must credit Robert J. Dingley, former president of the historical society, for bringing the wayward Chinese statue back to Naples.

He made it his top priority to retrieve the exotic treasure for the town. In 1971, with all the proper proofs in place, Mr. Dingley personally drove it—without incident, I might add—from the Boston Museum of Fine Arts to its present home at the Naples Historical Society museum.

Apparently it's the only one of its kind in New England. And its strange story is a one-of-a-kind tale: The original owners died suspiciously. Bad luck, unhappiness, tragedy, and premature death stalked all ensuing owners of Serenity Hill.

The only thing that is not mysterious about this tale is the idol's secure place in Naples's minimum-security museum. It was stolen once; would anyone dare steal it again?

# HAUNTED WATERS

*Abenaki Indians made pilgrimages to the Brunswick mineral springs
for healing, but always during the day. They never camped
overnight. The spirits, they believed, had a demonic side.*

—Tim Matson, *Round-Trip to Deadsville*

## A TRUE WONDER

Recently some friends asked me to show them the
Brunswick Springs.

I wasn't sure it was a good idea. The springs are saturated in
mystery, hidden away in the remotest portion of the state, and
possibly hazardous. Many dark and dangerous events have
happened there. After all, the springs are known to be cursed.

Would a trip deep into Vermont's fabled Northeast
Kingdom be putting my friends—and me—in harm's way?

Maybe. Still, I could understand their curiosity: The
Brunswick Springs form part of a haunted landscape, a mystical
hybrid of natural beauty, modern mystery, native history, and
ancient magic.

In fact, according to no less an authority than Robert Ripley,
the Brunswick Springs are the Eighth Wonder of the World . . .
*Believe It or Not.*

Mr. Ripley deemed them a "wonder" because they're a true
geologic anomaly: six individual springs forming a 15-foot
semicircle and bubbling from a single knoll. Though nearly as

close together as spigots on a soda fountain, the mineral content of each spring is completely different from that of its neighbor. Moving left to right, they are: Iron, Calcium, Magnesium, White Sulfur, Bromide, and—if you're brave enough—Arsenic. They flow from a steep bank just below the crest of a hill, then merge and drain into the Connecticut River, some 65 feet below.

## MEDICINE WATERS

To the Native Americans, the Brunswick Springs have always been magical healing waters located on sacred terrain. Though the Indians were displaced for a while by American commerce, the springs and their verdant surroundings retain a palpable air of otherworldliness.

This is a legend-crowded land. Before Europeons came, Abenakis made long-distance healing pilgrimages to the springs to partake of their "Medicine Waters of the Great Spirit."

It is important to add, however, that they only visited during the day, never remaining overnight. They saw it as a spiritual place, a natural place—but there was a night side to that nature, and evil was known to lurk after the sun went down. The Abenakis believed that powerful supernatural forces—light and dark—resided there. And either could be summoned.

Later, Europeans contributed their own set of myths.

For example, many still believe that a remnant of Rogers's Rangers stopped nearby on their retreat from the St. Francis raid. In a fireless and foodless campsite, fearing imminent onslaught from their French and Indian pursuers, they may have unloaded part of their pilfered treasure, burying it somewhere on the grounds. Over the years many holes have been dug, but—so far as I know—no treasure has been found.

A body of water on the premises is called Silver Lake. *Lake* may seem an overly generous designation; it's more like a tranquil pond. But lake, pond, or pool, legend says it's bottomless.

Ghosts are often reported in the vicinity. Some say Indian spirits dance silently upon Silver Lake's surface. More recently a woman drove her car into the water and drowned. Supposedly her spirit lingers there by the pool.

Over the years a few troubled souls have sought the springs' solitude to hang themselves. A nameless infant was found strangled to death and abandoned. In 1997 the crazed multiple murderer Carl Drega was cut down by police bullets near these haunted waters—evidence, some say, of their cleansing powers.

All in all, Brunswick Springs can be a spooky place.

More so at night.

And especially for those who know about the curse.

## WORDS AND WARFARE

The curse of the Brunswick Springs began when America was young and ran its course until the end of the twentieth century.

Though marvelous tales had been circulating among Native Americans for centuries, the springs' first historically documented miracle happened in 1784, when Indians from the Canadian end of Lake Memphremagog transported a wounded British soldier to the site. He had an injured arm; lifeless and badly damaged, he feared he might lose it to infection or the surgeon's saw. An Abenaki shaman positioned the soldier beneath the Medicine Waters, allowing their mineral streams to converge according to some long-forgotten formula. Though the subtleties of the incident are lost, history records one thing for sure: Life returned to the stricken limb.

The progression of events over the next century is vague and confusing.

Brunswick—chartered in 1761—and the towns around it were never densely populated. But settlers did trickle in, a few at a time. Then, as now, the springs were the local wonder. Indian and Anglo took freely of their waters. In time, however, the notion of free sharing began to erode, replaced eventually by free enterprise. Early American entrepreneurs saw financial opportunity in the magical waters.

Businessmen bargained. Offers were made. But Native Americans held firm, refusing to sell what nature gave for free.

It was not long before this economic tension led to fighting. Two Indians were killed.

The mother of one, a shaman, retaliated with words that must have been uttered at night, words that would be long remembered: "Any use of the waters of the Great Spirit for profit *will never prosper.*" They have echoed ominously over the centuries, but their full impact as a curse would be slow in coming.

## BUSINESS IS BOOMING

As Native Americans vanished from the land, the springs' reputation continued to grow.

In 1790 one Major French opened a boardinghouse nearby to provide travelers convenient access to the marvelous waters. He charged for meals and lodging, but use of the waters remained free to all.

In 1800 David Hyde turned his home into a sort of bed-and-breakfast establishment. The enterprise did so well that David was able to expand in 1815. He prospered, but only as an innkeeper; he didn't sell the waters.

By 1820 twelve neighboring families on both sides of the Connecticut River got in on the act, opening their homes to "city boarders."

Still the Great Spirit's miracle waters remained free for the taking. And their fame increased. They became renowned for curing such exotic ailments as dyspepsia, scrofula, salt rheum, lifeless limbs, and loss of vitality. Their ability to relieve kidney problems, consumption, rheumatism, and glandular troubles was legendary.

By 1845 the sick, the curious, and the skeptics were making the difficult journey by stage, horse, and on foot from as far away as Portland, Maine, to sample Vermont's healing springs.

Then, in the mid–nineteenth century, an event occurred that changed the economic face of Vermont. Railroads spread their iron arteries throughout the state, making trips to the springs almost effortless.

In 1860 accommodations for travelers changed from rustic to regal when Charles Bailey erected the first official hotel near the springs. He sold it at a considerable profit to local dentist D. C. Rowell.

Dr. Rowell renamed his hotel the Brunswick Spring House.

Fate seemed to smile on the good doctor as year after year his guest rooms filled to capacity. Timing was part of it. All over the world mineral waters were growing in popularity, and he had the railroad delivering passengers almost to his door.

But eventually the enterprising dentist made a fatal mistake: He opened a bottling plant. For the first time in the history of the springs, the waters were for sale.

Perhaps the Great Spirit of the Abenakis knew that the end had come—that finally the magical waters would be forever lost to all but the wealthy.

In 1894—as if it were some kind of supernatural warning shot—the Brunswick Spring House burned to the ground.

But Dr. Rowell was not quick to give up his gold mine. He rebuilt his hotel, calling the new operation Pine Crest Lodge. Perhaps, remembering what people had told him about the

curse, he discontinued his bottling operation; we don't know for sure. In fact, any misfortunes that befell him are unrecorded, so we must conclude that he prospered until he died in 1910.

## THE TWENTIETH CENTURY

With the beginning of the twentieth century, the hotel was once again for sale. Businessmen from all around greedily eyed the watery enterprise.

With nothing to look forward to but American avarice and exploitation, it seems the Great Spirit had had enough. The fatal countdown began. Brunswick's worst collisions with the supernatural were about to occur.

John Corbin Hutchins of nearby North Stratford, New Hampshire, looked at the springs and saw a shining vision of economic triumph. Then again, John was a man of vision. He was a successful druggist, real estate agent, and mortician, so he already had most of his financial bases covered.

In many ways John was the perfect picture of an early-twentieth-century businessman. A larger-than-life character with an all-consuming appetite for recognition and a talent for self-promotion, his mantra seemed to be *More*.

In addition to everything else, he developed a lucrative business buying up huge tracts of north country woodland, establishing himself as a lumber baron of wide renown.

But when it came to the arena of politics, John C. Hutchins was less successful. In local and statewide elections, he consistently fell just short of fame. His inability to succeed politically should have warned him not to challenge "higher powers," but when he saw the Brunswick Springs, he turned a blind eye and would brook no talk of curses.

Objectively, the springs seemed a good, safe investment, located as they were just a short auto trip from the Hutchins building, his seat of power in North Stratford. Acquiring them was a sensible extension of two of his businesses—real estate and pharmaceuticals. In addition to running a hotel, he could sell cords of lumber and cases of nature's "magic elixir."

His logic was no doubt sound. All over the world grand resorts were prospering solely because of their weird-tasting water. Here—easily within his grasp—was something extraordinary. Anyone could see the Brunswick Springs composed a beautiful picture, framed by the Connecticut River, the magnificent White Mountains, a tiny sparkling lake, and the lovely Green Mountains of Vermont. It was an entrepreneurial dream come true!

With Robert Ripley providing international awareness, and with the railroad transporting hordes of health seekers to his door, how could he possibly lose?

John C. Hutchins bought the place.

He lavished a considerable fortune simply marketing his resort. An extravagant color pamphlet was printed and widely distributed, emphasizing the springs' Native American mystique. Its cover proclaimed, "Medicine Waters of the Great Spirit!" showing a kneeling brave partaking of the magic fountain. Needless to say, there was no mention of the celebrated Indian curse; employees were instructed never to discuss it.

In effect John had gone head-to-head with the springs' supernatural protector.

Big mistake. On September 19, 1929, his brand-new Brunswick Springs Hotel burned to the ground. It was gone before it opened its doors, before its first guest had checked in.

But of course these things happen, right?

How could it be anything but a freak accident?

John C. Hutchins wasn't the kind of man who'd give up on

a good thing, not when he could turn apparent misfortune into opportunity. He wasted no time deciding to replace the ruins with a bigger and better resort. This time he would go all-out, build a grand hotel! A showpiece!

A local contractor with the unlikely name of Harry Savage drove his crew through the long, harsh winter months. A true Yankee, Mr. Savage proved as good as his word: By springtime the new hotel was ready to open its doors.

What a place it was! Northern Vermont had never seen anything like it: four and a half stories high with one hundred rooms, huge plate-glass windows, and a 155-foot piazza offering spectacular panoramic views of the Connecticut River and the Green Mountains' splendor.

A polished staff was recruited, including uniformed chauffeurs to drive two brand-new Packard limousines whose sole purpose to transport guests to and from the railroad station.

Reservations poured in.

But in a supernatural sense, it was all for naught. On May 15, 1930—just one month before the new hotel was to officially open—the night watchman spotted smoke billowing from a storage room. Before he could run and call for help, superheated phone lines stretched and snapped, cutting him off from the rest of the world.

Flames raged through the rooms like an angry army of demons. By midday it was over. John's grand hotel was once again nothing but a cremated corpse, a twisted skeleton of blackened pipes and smoldering timbers.

Some said this time the Great Spirit had surely finished him off. But John didn't believe in warnings from the spirit world. Above all, he was no quitter. Two fires in two years were not enough to discourage him. The stubborn Mr. Hutchins was determined to build again.

~

## ROUND THREE

Contractor Savage's crew was in practice. The foundation was already in place. Again they worked through the winter and the new hotel went up with comparative ease.

By the spring of 1931, John's latest masterwork was ready for business.

The new building had a few more rooms than its predecessor, more than half of them with private baths. And—included in the price—Brunswick Spring water was pumped into every room.

The exterior design was the same, but finished with the stucco that was currently in vogue.

The only thing John had forgotten—or had chosen to ignore—was the curse: "Any use of the waters of the Great Spirit for profit will never prosper."

On April 23, 1931, John C. Hutchins's third and last hotel was struck down by preternatural fire and burned to the ground. The local *Coos County Democrat* newspaper spread the word throughout the area: "Fire Again Levels New Hotel! Beautiful Brunswick Springs Structure, The Second New Hotel on Spot to Be Burned Within Year."

Apparently this time John got the message. Maybe he even became a believer. In any event, he never tried again.

And in the seventy years that have followed, neither has anyone else.

## A FINAL BLOW

By any stretch of the imagination, the unfortunate Mr. Hutchins's indomitable hubris put him in direct conflict with a will far more powerful than his own.

According to Charles Jordan's book *Tales Told in the Shadows of the White Mountains*, John C. Hutchins may well have been the last victim of the Curse of the Brunswick Springs—a curse that pursued him even after death.

Before his last hotel had stopped smoldering, John was in the hospital. His health continued to decline steadily until March 22, 1938, when, at age seventy-four, he passed away.

But the ultimate blow was yet to come.

Mr. Jordan was there to witness the last act of the tragedy. He writes, "In many ways, the curse of the springs became the curse of John C. Hutchins—a bad-luck streak which strangely reemerged in 1995 . . . [when] a line of freight trains derailed just as they had crossed into North Stratford, plowing into the Hutchins building." Eight days later, as the toppled railcars were pulled away, Mr. Jordan was watching. "The first floor began buckling, as if the building were quaking to life on its own. The second floor lurched forward, the back end of the structure dropped and the building collapsed onto itself in a huge cloud of dust. I had witnessed—and photographed—the last tragedy of John Corbin Hutchins."

## AUTHOR'S NOTE

My three friends repeatedly asked me to guide them to the Brunswick Springs. Even after I'd told the story and explained the hazards, they remained determined.

"I can't guarantee what'll happen out there," I told them. "But don't even joke about selling the water."

We set out early from my home in Burlington; it would be more than a three-hour trip. There's no direct route across the state and north along the Connecticut River into Vermont's own version of "The Outer Limits."

Finally—hot and already exhausted—we stopped at the tiny Brunswick Town Hall on the eastern side of Route 102. There were no other cars around—there never are—so we took our gear, climbed over the gate, and followed the path leading into the woods behind the building.

I warned my companions that it would be a good long walk, but even that did not discourage them.

Bright noonday sun beat down on a canopy of green leaves, flooding us in a surreal emerald half-light. It was easy to imagine ourselves as pioneers making our way up the Connecticut Valley, plunging deeper into the unknown, looking for a place to camp or call home.

Before we'd walked a quarter mile, we were perspiring profusely.

Lauren said, "We should have brought canteens."

Lenny and I laughed. "There's six springs up ahead," Lenny said.

"And if you're still thirsty," I added, "there's the whole Connecticut River."

Laughter, forced from the start, died away to utter silence. Finally Diane said, "We should have thought to bring a camera."

"And some tobacco," said Lenny. None of us smoked, but I knew what he meant. Tobacco is a proper offering to the Native Americans. And to their spirits. If we planned to take some of the springwater, we should be prepared to leave something in return.

As resident ghost expert, it became my job to tell them tales as we moved along the grassy path that had once been a road. Birdcalls and an occasional skittering in the bushes kept us looking from side to side. An intermittent, errant wind lent atmosphere to my stories.

"So, do you believe in the curse?" Lauren asked.

I pretended I didn't hear. Instead, I told them about the magnificent vision some campers claimed to have seen upon the waters of Silver Lake. A gigantic Indian, in full headdress regalia, mounted on a rearing stallion. It glowed brilliantly against the night sky and reflected in the still water's mirror-like surface.

Lenny wasn't buying it. "That sounds like a Plains Indian, not an Abenaki," he said. And he was right. But that is also the nature of certain visions: If you are supposed to see an Indian, you will see the one who's in your head.

By the time we began to skirt the shore of Silver Lake, I was walking with Diane; Lenny and Lauren lagged somewhere behind us. We could hear them talking quietly whenever the breeze subsided.

When I began to detect the faint odor of sulfur, I knew we were getting close. I led Diane to the left, cutting through the woods toward the springs.

Suddenly we both stopped and looked at each other. Lenny and Lauren stopped too. All at once everything was absolutely still. No breeze. No animals. No birdsong. No rushing water. It was as if we had suddenly plunged into an eerie vacuum.

Later, comparing notes, we realized that each of us had felt exactly the same thing at the same time: the overwhelming sensation that we were not alone.

Diane glanced around. Soon her gaze froze as she peered into a dark recess of shadows among the poplars, just across the trail from Silver Lake. I looked, too, and wondered if she saw what I was seeing.

There, beside the black, gnarly trunk of some ancient tree, I clearly saw the face of an Indian. His beardless features, his long black hair, his absolute stillness, made me think I was seeing exactly what those doomed Rangers had feared so very long ago.

I blinked repeatedly, but the vision did not go away. This was no fantasy of light and shadow. He was there, all right. Man or apparition, I couldn't tell, but he was there.

Diane moved closer to me as I backed up ever so slightly.

In a situation like this, people seem to intuit things: knowledge gained without words. Somehow, I knew he had been with us from the start. He'd probably been observing us from the moment we left our cars.

I tried to suppress the fear that was tightening the muscles of my abdomen.

He stepped out of the shadows, began moving slowly forward. He never blinked, walking, it seemed, as if he were in a trance. Something was in his hand. A gun, I thought. But it wasn't a gun, it was a tomahawk.

And now he was getting closer.

His expression was severe, inscrutable. He never broke eye contact.

When he was within twenty feet, I discerned that his tomahawk was in fact a hatchet.

Now he was 10 feet away. I was relieved that his hatchet never left his side.

I took a step toward him, Diane still at my side. Lauren and Lenny approached, too.

The man—dressed in blue jeans and kind of rough looking—

was obviously at home here. Although this land had been commercially developed for a while, it had been neglected for more than half a century until, in 1992, it once again became the property of the Abenaki Nation.

So this was his land. We were the trespassers.

Lenny, who has a disarming informality about him, stepped right up to the stranger. He smiled as if they were old friends and was the first to break the silence. Looking at the hatchet, he said, "You going to chop a few trees?"

The man didn't smile. He didn't answer. He didn't raise his hatchet. Our tension was still colored by a sense of unrelieved menace.

Finally, as if having decided which language to address us in, he spoke "No. I'm just cleaning up a little. I'm sort of the caretaker here. Been at it ten years now."

Lenny introduced himself and his wife, then he introduced Diane and me.

Conversation stopped. The man locked a contemptuous gaze on me. "I've heard of you," he said, "Joe Citro. You've written about this place. You published pictures. That isn't right. This is a sacred place, you know. Not some tourist spot. Not for pictures."

Still keeping his ax in my peripheral vision, I tried to set the record straight. "You're right," I told him, "I *have* written about the springs. But I never took pictures. In fact, I've never even brought a camera in here. I know there are pictures out there. I've seen lots of them. But I didn't take them."

He stared at me. Finally he acknowledged my words with a brief, stiff nod. There was to be no argument. I had told him the truth, and he believed me.

"You want me to show you around?" he said.

"That would be great."

First, in turn, he made each of us experience a purification ceremony. We sat on the ground, cross-legged, as he burned a sprig of sage, letting the pungent vapors pass over us. "This will protect you," he said.

We didn't ask from what.

Then he led us around the ancient foundation of a ruined hotel. In one corner he showed us a pile of multicolored glass shards and empty bottles. Beer bottles. "I've cleaned all this up," he said. "Kids come in here. They make a mess of the place. Leave their trash behind. We don't mind if people come here; this is a place for everyone. But they should treat it with respect. They wouldn't drink beer and smash bottles in a church. They shouldn't do it here. It isn't right. This place is older than their churches."

He led us to the top of a rise from which we could see a broad stretch of the Connecticut River gently flowing south. He described how his people once came here by water and by land. They'd visit every summer from the far reaches of Canada. They'd raise corn on the intervales, fish for salmon and trout, and hunt the plentiful game in the surrounding forests.

And of course they'd bring their sick to the springs—Nebisonbik, he called them, meaning "mineral water place." Certain elders, he said, were ailing so badly they had to be carried. But the springs would cure them.

"Can we see the springs?" Diane said.

"Come on."

He led us down crumbling concrete stairs toward the river. The years had chipped away at them and the adjoining cement walkway that gave access to six springs. Rusty pipes embedded horizontally in the concrete took care of the overflow. Excess water drained through them, spilling down toward the Connecticut.

A block of the cement structure had broken away and tumbled halfway down the bank. It was the size of a washing machine.

He made no apologies for the way things looked. The ruins were the work of white entrepreneurs. Nature was well along in its restoration process.

"Each spring is different," he said. "In the right combination, they can cure any disease. You gotta know how to mix them, but all the medicine you'd ever need is right here."

I was hoping—I think all of us were hoping—he'd tell us the Abenaki version of the curse story. But somehow it didn't seem right to ask.

I looked around at the pools and pipes, examined the dark, damp, mossy-smelling earth surrounding the springs. Other visitors had left totems near the water: coins, medals, beads, a pouch of Red Man chewing tobacco, feathers, photographs, a pocketknife, and some mysterious tiny, tightly wrapped packets containing . . . what? We didn't know and we didn't ask.

My Roman Catholic upbringing made me think of offerings at an altar.

"These waters come a great way underground," he told us. "See, the flow is the same. Summer, winter, drought, flood season, the flow is the same."

We nodded like students on a field trip.

"There's only a four-degree difference in temperature summer and winter," he said.

The smell of sulfur was strong but not unpleasant. The ground directly beneath the drainpipes was a dull rainbow, dyed by multicolored minerals.

One square hole contained white stringy mineral deposits that I couldn't identify. Strands swayed like hair in the current. I felt like a jerk when the thought *scalps* entered my head. The notion vanished: my own stupid biases flowing away with the springwater.

We followed his gaze as he looked down across the waters of the Connecticut River. "I can see this land, the springs, the fields by the river, all full with our people. Hundreds of them. The people. The animals. The land. I can see it just the way it was before your people came."

And—just for that moment—I think we could see it, too.

Now he didn't have to tell us about their version of the curse. We knew.

By the time we said good-bye, we were all friends. The threat—and there never had been a threat—was all in our imagination.

He invited us to return, reminding us that this place was for everyone.

Before we knew it, he had faded back into the trees and vanished.

## A LOOK AT THE FUTURE

As we enter the twenty-first century, there isn't much left of the once grand structures around Brunswick Springs. Even the locals can't tell you everything that's happened here. In general, the strange legends of fire and water have faded from memory.

Though the buildings are gone, the magical waters continue to flow, just as they have for thousands upon thousands of years, spreading their peculiar red, white, and blue mineral trail across an odd bit of American history. That ancient, unnamed sorceress was correct: No one has ever exploited these waters for long. As we drove home, all seemed right. The Abenaki Nation has reacquired the springs, Silver Lake, and a hundred acres of surrounding woodland.

Today, and I hope for all time, the Brunswick Springs, the "Medicine Waters of the Great Spirit"—Nebisonbik—once again flow free for all to share.

# A SHADOW OVER CROMPTON

*The manifestations were evident over many years, and old-time residents always felt something strange about the lovely old church on the hillside above the Velvet Village.*

–Fr. Edmund H. Fitzgerald

## IN THE LAND OF LOVECRAFT

Rhode Island is supernatural country, according to native writer H. P. Lovecraft. For some, it's the horror capital of New England. This tiny state with the big name (State of Rhode Island and Providence Plantation) is seemingly filled with monsters, ghosts, and vampires.

Still, what should perhaps be nicknamed the "Eldritch State" seems strangely bereft of curses. You'd almost suspect some kind of cover-up or conspiracy. Maybe something far more sinister is at work: Could the whole state be cursed?

Mr. Lovecraft only hints at such arcane possibilities.

Luckily, Providence's Bard of the Blasphemous never discovered the little town of Crompton; he saved it for me.

This out-of-the-way New England village, with many Old English characteristics, claims an infernal incident that is not only unique, but also—according to at least one unimpeachable source—transmits its eerie echoes to this very day.

Yes, there is a curse. And a good deal more than that. Mr. Lovecraft would have loved it.

But first the history . . .

~

## FROM STONE TO VELVET

The town of Crompton—part of today's West Warwick—was developed in 1807, carved out of a heavily wooded area near the south branch of the Flat (aka Pawtuxet) River. On twenty acres of land, the Providence Manufacturing Company constructed its first cotton mill. Because it was made from locally quarried granite, they called it Stone Mill. In fact, for a time the village itself was called Stone Factory.

But when manufacturing began, the nearby farm families employed there, unaccustomed to such confining quarters—referred to their building as the Stone Jug.

Around 1816, for reasons too convoluted to analyze, the mill folded. It shut down and stood vacant for about five years until it was reopened by a new group of investors. They called themselves the Crompton Company in honor of James Crompton, an English mill owner and designer of machinery, who had visited the area in 1820. He rendered such invaluable advice on improving machinery and production that apparently his counsel saved not only the mill but also the town itself. In his honor the village of Stone Factory was renamed Crompton.

The new Cromptom Mill rapidly improved production. Soon it distinguished itself by being the first company in the United States to manufacture velvet and corduroy. So much in demand were these pleasing textiles that Crompton became known as the Velvet Village. When other mills caught on and Crompton was no longer the products' sole producer, the town remained the best producer, winning many awards for its fine fabric.

As business grew, more workers were needed. The scattered cottages and farms of the area could supply only a finite quantity of sturdy Anglo-Puritan employees.

Beginning in the early 1840s, a large group of Irish immigrants settled in Crompton, escaping the homeland potato famine and trying to establish new lives in the land of plenty. Many were skilled weavers, dyers, and cloth printers who easily secured work in the mill. A highly religious group, these Irish Catholics had to walk, in a gradually growing group, all the way to Saints Peter and Paul Church (now the Cathedral) in Providence—a distance of some 10 miles—to attend Mass. Soon, enough Catholics had settled in the Velvet Village to want a church of their own.

## OPPOSING FORCES

But there was a lot of anti-Irish, anti-Catholic sentiment in the area, enough to make the simple matter of building a church absurdly complex. First, and perhaps most vexing, no one would sell them the land on which to build.

The Catholics secretly contrived a simple plan. A sympathetic English couple in the village, Paul and Mary Doran, agreed to buy the land as if expanding their own holdings. Paul was a skilled block printer, earned good wages, and had put some money away. Mary independently raised enough to supplement the Dorans' contribution.

The deal was struck.

Then the Dorans surprised everyone by deeding their one-acre lot to the Roman Catholic bishop of Hartford (who was living in Providence). That done, the "papists" finally had a foothold in town. Now it looked as if the Crompton Catholics would have their place of worship after all.

But there were still forces at work that intended to keep Catholicism at bay. Someone—it is not known who—made a preternatural pronouncement, declaring, "The first man to break ground for the Catholic church will die a sudden death."

Perhaps it was a scare tactic, perhaps the work of a sorcerer, or a black magician, but as knowledge of the curse spread among the superstitious Irish, planning continued...but progress stopped.

It's easy to picture a group of hardy Irishmen standing on what would become the church grounds, picks and shovels in hand, exchanging words, lighting pipes, sipping beverages, looking at each other—no one daring to make the first move.

## CHEATING THE DEVIL?

Finally, in 1844, Paul Doran, who had donated the land, hit upon another simple scheme. "Look," he said to the assembled work crew, "you know the words of the curse as well as I do: 'The first man to break ground for the church will die a sudden death.'"

He had the crowd's attention; all eyes stared expectantly at him.

"The curse clearly says, 'the first *man*,'" he continued, emphasizing the word. "My wife, Mary—whom I assure you is no man—has volunteered to break ground so our work here may begin."

It was an inventive solution. The assembled workers cheered as Paul Doran made a big show of handing a spade to his wife.

With equal flourish Mary plunged the spade to the ground, modestly hiked up her skirt just a bit, and used her thick-soled shoe to drive the shovel into the earth.

Nothing happened. The ground was much too hard. A laborer nearby handed her a crowbar with which she vigorously hacked at the earth, leaving a deep gash. At last, church ground was broken!

But perhaps the effort was too much for her.

For a moment Mary Doran stood there wide-eyed, as if something unseen had slapped her soundly on the backside. Then, slumping a little at the knees, she clutched the crowbar as if it were a cane. She tried to remain standing, but her legs wouldn't hold. Rushing forward, her husband grabbed her just as she began to fall. He lowered her gently to the earth, where she died moments later in his arms.

Perhaps this is, in part, why they called it St. Mary's Catholic Church. Mary Doran's bravery and sacrifice made possible the building of the small wooden church where the Irish, and soon the French Canadians, could worship. F. James Gibson became the first resident priest. For years it was known far and wide as "the Irish Church."

Mary Hodson Doran was to be the first person buried in the churchyard within the land that she and her husband had donated. Her gravestone records that she was thirty-three years old at the time of her death.

## SIGNS

Today St. Mary's is recognized as the first Catholic church in Rhode Island to be built outside the cities of Providence, Pawtucket, or Newport. It is therefore one of the oldest in the state.

It is also recognized for Mary Doran's sacrifice and for the generosity she and her husband showed the community.

But St. Mary's is known for something else. There has long been a peculiar, eerie air that pervades the church and grounds. People in the area remember avoiding the place as children, saying it made them uncomfortable.

Old-timers have always been aware of something inexplicably tense in the church's atmosphere—something they can't precisely define. Whatever it is seems at odds with the church's quaint and scenic Old English facade.

Apparently a ghostly presence haunts St. Mary's Church— one not to be confused with the Holy Spirit.

Even today certain church council members will not go into St. Mary's alone at night.

It is as if Mary Doran gave up more than her life to that fatal curse so many years ago. It is as if she gave something of her soul as well, for that nondescript presence is widely accepted to be the ghost of Mary Doran herself.

Many townsfolk and parishioners have had run-ins with the mysterious shade. Over time, a body of unexplained phenomena has accumulated suggesting that St. Mary's Church may be one of the most haunted places in all Rhode Island.

## UNIMPEACHABLE PROOF

I have in my possession an affidavit signed by Fr. Edmund H. Fitzgerald, Ph.D., dated August 19, 2002. Father Fitzgerald was pastor of St. Mary's from 1984 to 1992; his doctorate is in colonial history.

In his statement he enumerates a number of manifestations that he has personally experienced during his tenure. These show how he became convinced that the spirit of the church is, in fact, Mary Doran.

In 2003 I interviewed him at length to review each incident.

Father Fitzgerald frequently heard footsteps—presumably a woman's—on the hard red cedar floorboards of the old church. "It sounded like they were right behind me," he said. "But I was alone in the church. I'd turn around. No one would be there."

"One Christmas Eve [in 1989 or 1990]," he writes, "following the Mass of the Christ Child, the tower bell rang of its own accord after the congregation left the church grounds. Even recent hurricanes did not cause the bell to ring in this way."

This timely tolling occurred at around 5:00 P.M. while Father Fitzgerald was leaving and locking the door. When he went back to investigate, he says, "The bell rope was moving up and down all by itself, but there was nobody in the church. That bell can only ring from someone pulling the rope."

I asked him why he supposed it happened.

"What better time for it to ring?" he said "To celebrate the birth of the Christ Child!"

Perhaps equally mysterious is the church organ that will, on occasion, play all by itself. Father Fitzgerald recalls a time it played after a funeral, "even though the instrument was closed, locked, and covered with its cloth. And the loft lights were extinguished."

He also experienced another peculiar incident involving holy water: "The rear sanctuary wall was being painted one Saturday by a father and son team (who never left the immediate area all day). Before the painting commenced, a Waterford bowl was emptied of water and removed from the altar. Later, upon completion of their work, when the painters returned it to its place on the altar, the bowl was found to be filled with water." Father Fitzgerald's report then discusses the testimonial commemorating St. Mary's seventieth anniversary. It had been hanging on the wall since 1914, framed in solid oak with double-thick glass. It was so heavy and secured so snugly that it would have been impossible for one person to move on his or her own. Indeed, it had never been removed before.

But somehow, Father Fitzgerald recalled, it moved all the same. Twice in one day. Unobserved. Unexplained.

It was easily discovered on a nearby ledge with its hooks still in place. There were no telltale marks or scratches. And no clues how or why such a heavy, cumbersome object might have moved on its own.

Most of Father Fitzgerald's meetings with the St. Mary's specter have been nonvisual—with one possible exception: Once, while standing inside the church looking out through a window, he saw a figure out of the corner of his eye. A figure standing right beside him. But when he turned his head, no one was there.

## AUTHOR'S NOTE

Though Father Fitzgerald says he never found his otherworldly experiences frightening, he is nonetheless convinced the church is haunted, and that the spirit is that of Mary Doran. At the same time, he dismisses the curse component of the story altogether, calling it "silly superstition."

So we are left with an odd imbalance. Is Mary Doran remaining as a caretaker spirit, forever watching over the church that she helped establish?

Or if she was in fact felled by an anti-Catholic curse, is she doomed to walk the "desecrated grounds" until Judgment Day?

I know of no way to answer this question. And I fear Mr. Lovecraft's explanation would be too horrible to contemplate.

# THE CRASH
# OF CAMELOT

*It was an ill-fated house. . . . A curse seemed to hang over the family,*
*making men sin in spite of themselves and bringing suffering and*
*death down upon the innocent as well as the guilty.*

–Edith Hamilton, *Mythology*

### THE KING OF CAMELOT

Joseph P. Kennedy was the perfect candidate for a curse. The
son of an East Boston Irish saloonkeeper-turned-politician,
Joe always had his eye unwaveringly fixed on greatness.
Specifically, he planned to become the president of the United
States.

Propelled by a craving for power, he enhanced his grandiose
vision more with an Irish-bred sense of sovereignty than with
American democratic ideals. For Joe Kennedy, siring an
American dynasty was a dream within reach.

But to enter the most powerful office in the world, Joe knew
he would require two essential keys: money and influence. He
therefore pursued these via any channel available to him, legal
and illegal. His résumé of curse-worthiness reads like a satanic
rap sheet. Here's the much-abbreviated version:

Though Joe was a poor student at the prestigious Boston
Latin School—he even had to repeat his final year—his father's
influence got him into Harvard when his grades would not.
There his academic career remained unremarkable, but he
quickly learned that influence would advance him more

readily than study. Joe deliberately became chummy with his professors, routinely supplying them with alcoholic gifts passed along from his father. This, and his minimal academic efforts, eventually graduated him from Harvard with one A, four Bs, nineteen Cs, and ten Ds (one of which was in Social Ethics).

When his athletic prowess was insufficient to earn him a Harvard baseball letter, Joe tried an alternate approach. The team's captain, he learned, planned to open a movie theater upon graduation. Joe persuaded some of his politically connected cronies to quietly inform the captain of the price of a theater license in Boston. Subsequently, Joe received his crimson sweater with its coveted black H.

By the time he had finished college, Joe had mastered the techniques of "influence" on his own. Now he was ready. He would start to configure his "American Kingdom," his vision of a Kennedy Camelot.

The daughter of Boston's mayor John "Honey Fitz" Fitzgerald was to be a prime addition to Joe Kennedy's domain. With Rose Fitzgerald as his queen, the Kennedy round table quickly began to fill up. Between 1915 and 1932 the couple produced five princesses and—in Joe's mind more important—four princes. Thus began the Kennedy dynasty.

While running his father's bank, Joe learned what Harvard had neglected to teach him: how to manipulate the stock market and acquire vast wealth from unsuspecting investors. He ruined a number of expendable pawns along the way.

His fortunes increased rapidly during Prohibition when he partnered up with infamous mobster Frank Costello, smuggling liquor from Canada and Cuba into the United States for distribution.

At this point he had mastered a simple economic principle: Money makes money.

## HOORAY FOR HOLLYWOOD!

By 1926 Joe Kennedy was unstoppable in his pursuit of his grandiose goals. Leaving his wife and family in Boston, he headed for California, where his marathon womanizing would go unchecked as his fortunes increased. Joe entered the movie business, purchasing the film company FBO (Film Booking Offices of America). He even started squiring Hollywood's hottest leading lady, Gloria Swanson.

Never content, he strove to increase and consolidate his power by taking over other studios and buying up theater chains.

When Alexander Pantages, an LA theater owner, resisted Joe's attempted monopoly, he was surprised to find a seventeen-year-old employee accusing him of rape. The befuddled theater owner was sentenced to fifty years in jail before the employee, Eunice Pringle, confessed that she had perjured herself because Joe Kennedy paid her $10,000 and promised to make her a movie star. She died shortly after going public. Though no autopsy was performed, the symptoms suggested cyanide poisoning.

For Camelot's patriarch, exploiting friendships and ruining lives was business as usual. It is likely a whole trail of damaged people cursed Joseph Kennedy's name.

## FDR AS STEPPING-STONE

Regardless of all resistance, professional or interpersonal, unrelenting ambition drove Joe Kennedy even harder. After pocketing some $500 million (in today's dollars) when he helped

orchestrate the 1929 crash of the stock market, he was finally ready to take his long-anticipated step into politics.

By helping Franklin Delano Roosevelt become elected president in 1932, Joe set himself up to collect a very big favor. Despite opposition from presidential advisers, Joe was able to bully his way into the ambassadorship of Great Britain, the first Irish U.S. ambassador to the Court of St. James. Considering the long-term tensions between Ireland and the British government, and considering Joe Kennedy's reputation for ill-timed bluntness and occasional belligerence, it was a risky and controversial appointment. After all, this was the most important diplomatic assignment in the world. The health of nations depended on it. But to Joe Kennedy, it was simply a short step away from the presidency in 1940.

It was no surprise to Kennedy critics that Joe soon committed blunders that would destroy his hopes of the White House forever.

One he did covertly. Embarrassed by the limited intelligence and potential of his oldest daughter, Rosemary, he feared she might make the wrong impression on the people he most needed to impress. Without consulting his wife, Joe had their daughter secretly lobotomized. The procedure went catastrophically wrong, and from age twenty-three the ruined woman passed her life behind the walls of St. Coletta's nursing convent in Wisconsin. She died in 2005.

His other sin was committed frequently and in the open. He went public with his admiration for Adolf Hitler and—as ambassador—failed to respond to reports of Nazi persecution of Jews. "Well, they brought it on themselves," he said of the powerless population in Hitler's Germany. In fact, he went so far as to predict that their persecutor would eventually overthrow England and possibly the United States. Not prudent prognostications from an ambassador in Britain with his eye on the American presidency.

Just before the outbreak of World War II, Ambassador Kennedy was returning to the United States on an ocean liner. Also aboard, fleeing the Nazis, was a poor Lubavitcher rabbi and six of his yeshiva students.

Bearded, long-haired, and black-clad, the Jews were praying on their holy day, Rosh Hashanah.

When Roman Catholic ambassador Kennedy observed them at their worship, he took offense. Straightaway, he complained to the ship's captain, saying the Jews were upsetting the first-class passengers. They should, he said, be made to stop conducting their rituals in front of other people.

In retaliation, Rabbi Israel Jacobson laid a curse on the arrogant American, damning him and all his male offspring to tragic fates.

And so it began ...

## THE COMING OF THE CURSE

According to Kennedy biographer Edward Klein, "In the forty years since the assassination of President John F. Kennedy, tragedy has struck the Kennedys and those associated with the family on the average of nearly once every two years."

True, but the family's sinister saga did not commence with JFK. The Kennedy Curse, brought on by Joseph P. Kennedy's destructive ambition and colossal insensitivity, began—just as Rabbi Jacobson said—with the now forgotten Kennedy male, Joe's eldest son, Joe Jr. Then, from oldest to youngest, it ran its course through the family.

## FIRSTBORN SON

Born in 1915, Joseph Patrick Kennedy Jr. died just before his thirtieth birthday.

Typical of the Kennedy profile, he was attractive, intelligent, fiercely competitive, privileged, promiscuous, and prone to put-downs in his humor, a habit often described as his "mean streak."

Since Joe Sr. had destroyed his own chances for the presidency, he intended to place his first son in the White House. He plotted Joe's path step by step. First, a Harvard education was essential. While his classmates smoked cigarettes to demonstrate their sophistication, Joe Jr. puffed away on Cuban cigars and boasted that he was destined to become the country's first Irish Catholic president.

Joe Jr. and his younger brother Jack (born 1917) enlisted in the navy after Pearl Harbor. Military credentials were, after all, essential to the résumé of a president. But fate was at odds with Father Joe's plans. Turns out it was the younger Kennedy, JFK, who became the hero, thanks to the PT 109.

Knowing his White House ambitions would be enhanced by the title "war hero," Joe Jr. was at a loss, suddenly eclipsed in the media and outranked in the military by his younger sibling.

The competitive spirit of the Kennedy brothers, long encouraged and reinforced by Father Joe, kicked in. Somehow Joe Jr. would have to outshine brother Jack.

There wasn't much time. The war was almost over; young Joe had to do something fast. In 1944 he volunteered for a dangerous flying mission rather than return stateside when his tour of duty ended.

With 23,562 pounds of Torpex—an explosive twice as powerful as TNT—packed into a bomber, Joe took the controls and was airborne. The plan was for the crew to parachute to safety while the explosives went on to destroy a V2 launch site in Normandy.

But something went terribly wrong. Joe's plane exploded in midair. Joseph Kennedy Jr. died in the flash and roar of ten tons of Torpex, at that time the biggest bomb the world had ever seen.

## JFK

Now it was Father Joe's second son on the presidential path.

As a youth, John Fitzgerald Kennedy spent four years at Choate, a prestigious prep school in Wallingford, Connecticut. He was frequently sick, missing a lot of class time. When well, Jack was an unremarkable student given to practical jokes and general tomfoolery. At one point he was even expelled for mocking the faculty. Father Joe's "persuasiveness" quickly got him reinstated.

But it was that mediocre student and general cutup who campaigned for the yearbook's highest honor, one traditionally reserved for serious students who exemplified Choate's loftiest ideals: "Most Likely to Succeed."

Jack was as likely to win that honor as he was to matriculate directly from Choate into Paradise. But in true Kennedy style—and as a parting bit of tomfoolery—he rallied his friends into his whimsical campaign, buying, trading, and cajoling votes. Though he knew he was undeserving, he won by a landslide.

Such victories—minor and major—were part of the Kennedy competitive makeup. Winning this seemingly small, yet strangely prophetic honor released Jack from the shadow of his older, recently graduated brother while maintaining his father's goodwill.

Later it was his father's money and influence that lubricated the sickly lad's way into the navy. Joe set up Jack's induction physical on "a personal favor basis," using insider help to locate a military doctor malleable enough to administer the kind of perfunctory examination Jack could pass.

It turned out to be a good move. After Joe Jr's death in 1944, old Joe Kennedy channeled 100 percent of his political ambitions through Jack. His second son became a U.S. representative (from 1947 to 1953) and a Massachusetts senator (1953 to 1960).

In 1953, responding to his father's command, JFK married Jacqueline Lee Bouvier, and "the American media family" was born. Jack and Jackie fully expected to live happily ever after—at least in the eyes of the American public.

But as we well know, theirs was to be a cursed union. Jack's inbred ambitions, compulsive womanizing, and chronic competitiveness would eventually lead to the most conspicuous of the many Kennedy tragedies.

It is a fact that mob connections—brokered through his bootlegger father—helped put JFK into the White House. Dealing with the Devil while living under a curse was to prove an exceedingly dangerous alchemy.

Turning away from his mob backers after winning the 1960 presidential election, then cracking down on organized crime, might have been incautious moves. But Jack—with typical Kennedy élan—thought he was invincible. After all, he had outshone his siblings, even one-upped his domineering father.

And he was used to such victories. While at Harvard Jack had taken great pleasure in finessing his way into the elite clubs his Irish father had never been permitted to join. And as president of the United States, his trophy conquest—Marilyn Monroe—outshone his father's dalliance with Gloria Swanson.

But forces were gathering that would culminate in Dallas, and JFK was too blind, too preoccupied, and far too distracted to anticipate any of them.

One wonders how a man in JFK's physical condition could have been such an effective president. When he took office, he was frequently out of commission with Addison's disease, a progressive glandular disorder whose symptoms include weakness, anemia, abnormal skin pigmentation (his famous tan), and weight loss. Its cause remains a mystery. Consequently, he was often in bed sick—or with a woman—while his public thought he was hard at work. Additionally, he suffered from back problems, the result of a birth defect in his spine. Chronic venereal disease was also in the picture. It infected his wife and caused the couple to lose children. Normally, the Catholic Kennedys had very big families.

But Jack was a master of media and self-promotional spin. He employed gifted image makers who knew how to capitalize on his million-dollar smile, agile wit, and preternaturally charming personality. As president, Jack Kennedy had as many worshipers as he did followers. Such a superhuman presence was primed for a fall.

And he had enemies ready to cheer when he crashed.

## NOVEMBER 22, 1963

In November 1963 President Kennedy ventured into what he called "nut country"—he went to Texas. There, powerful right-wingers were enraged by, among other things, his civil rights policies.

Still, he refused the protective bubble on his limousine as the presidential motorcade drove through the applauding hordes in downtown Dallas. Perhaps the last words he heard were spoken by Gov. John Connally's wife, who turned to him and said, "Mr. President, you certainly cannot say that Dallas doesn't love you." Then a volley of shots rang out.

It is beyond the scope of this chapter to speculate about lone gunmen versus dark conspiracies. The point is, the president was dead, and the Kennedy Curse continued.

At his funeral, Jack's brothers Robert and Ted marched with Jackie. Two male Kennedys down, two left standing.

## NEXT IN LINE

Robert may have been the first to consider the reality of a family curse. After Jack's death he took to reading Greek tragedies and contemplating the uncertainties of fate and the mysteries of his own future.

As attorney general of the United States and recipient of vast public sympathy and support, the forty-two-year-old father of eleven, Robert Francis Kennedy was perfectly positioned for the presidency. It was a logical ascendancy, and completely in accord with Father Joe's wishes.

At midnight on June 4, 1968, at the California Democratic campaign headquarters at the Ambassador Hotel in Los Angeles, his future was looking good.

Then, at 12:15 A.M., four shots rang out. Bobby was hit in the armpit and side but it was the bullet to his head that killed him. His last words were, "Jack. Jack."

As of June 5, 1968, Joseph Patrick Kennedy—now a helpless stroke-shattered invalid—had watched three of his four sons prematurely and unnaturally cut down just on the verge of greatness.

## AND THEN THERE WAS ONE

Today Ted, the youngest of King Joe's original round table, lives in the shadows of his legendary brothers, the shadow of the family curse, and the shadow of political superstardom he can never attain. As the last surviving male, this Kennedy son has been constantly under the public microscope, while misfortunes—many of his own making—have pursued him with demonic persistence.

He was expelled from Harvard for employing a friend to take an exam for him. In 1962 he began a long-term stint in the Senate that would never—and will never—lead to the White House. In 1964, on a flight to Springfield, Massachusetts, his small plane crashed, killing the pilot, the copilot, and an aide, but leaving Ted alive with a collapsed lung, fractured ribs, a broken back, and an elevated sense of his own mortality.

In 1968 his brother Bobby was murdered.

His next near hit came in 1969: the infamous Martha's Vineyard incident known simply as Chappaquiddick. That night Ted's car crashed off a bridge, leaving Mary Jo Kopechne drowned and Ted scurrying to avoid discovery. He waited ten hours before reporting the fatal accident. During that time he tried to persuade an in-law, Joe Gargan, to take the rap for him. In a speech after the Chappaquiddick incident, Ted speculated that "some awful curse" did actually hang over all the Kennedys.

Variously portrayed by the media as bloated buffoon or distinguished statesman, repeated public humiliation and near-death experiences must keep his dark, superstitious side on full alert. I wonder if "the curse" can ever be far from his thoughts.

Three miscarriages, a son who lost a leg to cancer, an alcoholic wife, a divorce, drug-damaged children, and a parade of mistresses cobble a path that is not likely to lead to greater things.

Perhaps the Kennedy Curse has already had its way with Ted. Or perhaps there are worse things waiting.

## THE WOMEN

Supposedly Rabbi Jacobson's curse was aimed only at Ambassador Joseph Kennedy's male children. But of Joe's nine offspring, only four were male.

What of the five women?

Rosemary, born in 1918, was eighty-six when she passed. More a victim of her father's curse than Rabbi Jacobson's, she spent her entire adult life institutionalized after the botched lobotomy.

Kathleen, born in 1920, died in 1948 at age twenty-eight. Another plane crash. Peter Fitzwilliam, her thirty-seven-year-old millionaire lover; the pilot; and the copilot died with her.

Born in 1921, Eunice seems, for the most part, to have avoided the slings and arrows of the family curse. Like her brother Jack, however, she has been continually plagued by an assortment of illnesses.

Patricia, born in 1924, married "Rat Packer" Peter Lawford in 1954, thus reattaching Kennedy glamour to Hollywood stardom. Pat was Peter's fourth wife. Any of the previous three could have warned her about Peter's bizarre sexual appetites, perverse predilections that didn't mix well with her strict Irish Catholic upbringing. Nor did his appetite for alcohol and multiple women. Though it can be argued that Peter Lawford was very like a typical Kennedy male, he wasn't the ideal match for a Kennedy woman. Their incompatibility led to divorce in 1962, after which Pat retreated to New York and escaped into booze and pills. Her children followed her example. She died in 2006.

Jean Ann, born in 1928, would pull the whole Kennedy clan together in defense of her son, William Kennedy Smith, when he was tried for rape in 1991.

## THE SINS OF THE FATHERS

The malignant tentacles of the Kennedy curse are evident in the children of Old Joe's brood, from the drug overdose death of Bobby's son David in 1984, to the scandalous spectacle of William Kennedy Smith's rape trial, to John Fitzgerald Kennedy Jr.'s 1999 plane crash, which also killed his wife, Carolyn, and her sister, Lauren Bessette.

And there's more. Joseph Kennedy II's Jeep accident in 1973, which left his girlfriend paralyzed and a man dead. Robert Kennedy Jr.'s heroin conviction in 1984. Patrick Kennedy's cocaine addiction in the 1980s. Michael Kennedy's Aspen, Colorado, ski death in 1997. Cousin Michael Skakel's murder conviction in 2002. And on and on and on...

I can't help but wonder if the suffering of the children is a continuation of the curse, or just further punishment for their parents, the original nine members of King Kennedy's round table.

## AUTHOR'S NOTE

When I began working on this book, I was dead set against including a chapter on the Kennedys. It seemed too tawdry, too salacious, altogether too tabloid. The last thing I wanted to do was create something more suitable for the supermarket scandal sheets.

But then I started looking at the facts. The odds. And the proliferation of misfortunes. Putting aside the assassinations, plane crashes alone have taken out Kennedy relatives at a rate of one every seven years for half a century!

I decided that writing a book about New England curses *without* including the Kennedys would be akin to writing a New England history and never mentioning Boston.

Outside the Greek tragedies, it is difficult to find a family more persistently plagued with grief and misfortune. Because the Kennedys are so like American royalty, their highs are higher, their lows are lower, and everything they do—public and private—eventually reaches the media's eye.

All evidence considered, it's easy to believe the Kennedy family is truly cursed. Robert believed it. So did Jackie and Ted. Their frequent family tragedies are far too numerous to chronicle in this short chapter; it would require a whole book. Luckily, one exists: Edward Klein's *The Kennedy Curse*.

Mr. Klein doesn't explain the family's difficulties solely in supernatural terms. He sees the "Kennedy Curse" as a tragic character flaw, one that is passed via genetics or upbringing from generation to generation, infecting family, in-laws, even acquaintances.

During an interview on CBS News in 2003, he said, "It's my view that the Kennedy family has what you might call a combination of classic hubris and modern genetics. They have this obsession with power, almost to the exclusion of ethical standards. This has led them to a feeling that they can get away with things that others can't . . . they're impelled to do self-destructive things."

He also believes the curse predates Joe Kennedy Sr., originating back in Ireland. He reminds us that the first Kennedy to arrive in America, Patrick, "came here with a terrible sense of inferiority and found more prejudice here. I think they compensated for that in some cases with this sort of grandiosity."

As I prepared this chapter, I wasn't able to completely disengage my admiration for JFK and Robert, nor my sympathies for a family so battered with pain, regardless of its source.

And so I can't bring my contemplation about the Kennedy dynasty to a comfortable closure. Are they an essentially corrupt family with a streak of greatness? Or a great family with a corrupt and corrupting core?

# A CLUSTER
# OF CURSES:
## AN EPILOGUE

Curses have been part of the New England landscape since before there were New Englanders. Though it would be impossible to include all of them in any single book, I have discovered that research on one inevitably discloses another. Sometimes several. *Cursed in New England*'s table of contents has the potential to be endless.

What follows is a sampling of New England curses that for me are still under investigation. Maybe you can add details to these, or contribute new curses to this ongoing roster.

For our quick final tour of the New England states, we'll begin in New Hampshire ...

## LITHOBOLIA

*Lithobolia, or The Stone Throwing Devil* is the title of a pamphlet written by Richard Chamberlain, onetime secretary for the colony of New Hampshire. It was published in England in 1698, though the events described took place on "Great Island"—part of Portsmouth, New Hampshire—in 1682.

Mr. Chamberlain gives a lengthy, detailed, and—perhaps most important—eyewitness account of peculiar events that beset the family and property of a prosperous Quaker farmer named George Walton.

For almost three months, bricks, stones, tools, and household implements bombarded the Waltons while also raining down on their home and outbuildings. No one was ever able to discover the source of the mysterious onslaught.

The Waltons quickly determined it was not the work of local jokesters when stones began to pelt them *inside* the house! Flying rocks from nowhere shattered glass and crockery, banged and rattled inside the chimney, and bounded along the floor like cannonballs.

Some, they discovered, felt hot, as if they had been taken from a fire.

The escalating madness continued day and night.

Wherever George went—to the barn, the field, or elsewhere—he was sure to receive a shower of stones . . . or something worse. Once an airborne sledgehammer narrowly missed his head.

It was evident that George was the primary target of the supernatural assault. But why?

Neighbors suspected his plight was the consequence of witchcraft. Apparently he had been cursed by an elderly woman, who maintained that George had cheated her out of a strip of land that was rightfully hers.

Prior to his witnessing the rockfall, Secretary Chamberlain was skeptical about witchcraft, but what he saw at the Walton home changed him. The incident, he wrote, "has confirmed myself and others in the opinion that there are such things as witches and the effects of witchcraft."

It is important to keep in mind that these events took place a good ten years prior to the hideous events in Salem, and may have helped pave the road that led to the Massachusetts madness.

# MOLLY OCKETT

Molly Ockett, an itinerant Abenaki healing woman, wandered the Upper Androscoggin and Connecticut Rivers. She dressed in the traditional Indian manner, including a pointed cap. Moving around as she did—through Maine, New Hampshire, Vermont, and parts of Canada—was the way of her people.

Her Indian name was Singing Bird, but the French Catholics had christened her Marie Agatha. It is likely she pronounced it *Mali Agget,* which became *Molly Ockett* to the English ear.

In 1759, at age fifteen, she apparently survived Rogers's Rangers attack on Odanak (St. Francis) by hiding in the bushes. Yet she seemed to hold no grudges.

Molly became well known for her many kindnesses, her good advice, and her peaceful ways. She was a colorful and much-loved visitor to many towns and homes. Because of her wandering lifestyle, a number of different towns were proud to claim her, especially in Maine.

She was particularly renowned for her ability to cure. In fact, she was the only doctor available to numerous white settlers in the northern wilds. She had an uncanny manner of showing up just when medical attention was needed. The list of people who owed Molly their lives is long and varied.

For example, around 1772 in the Upper Androscoggin, Molly treated Henry Tufts for a serious knife wound. In his journals, Henry referred to Molly as a "doctor." He learned what he could about Abenaki medicine. "In general," he wrote, "[Abenaki healers] were explicit in communication, still I thought them in possession of secrets they cared not to reveal."

What secrets could those have been?

In his book *Room for the Indians*, Dr. Robert Haldane Jr. wrote, "My maternal grandmother . . . told of Molly Ockett and others who had the power to bless or curse the future of an area. Molly cursed Snow Falls, and to this day, no business has long survived on that spot."

Curses seem out of character for this gentle and peaceful woman, but apparently she uttered a few, and they were just as effective as her cures.

During the hard winter of 1809, Molly Ockett was wandering in Maine, from Andover to Paris. A terrible, blinding blizzard seized the area and Molly soon became lost. She was forced to stop at the unfamiliar home of a newly settled miller in Snow Falls to ask directions. She also requested shelter for the night.

The miller, a stranger to the area, neither knew Molly nor understood the Abenakis' wandering ways. In short, he summarily turned her away, sending her back into the snowstorm.

Fatigued and furious, Molly is said to have used her magic in a rare demonstration of malevolence. She put a curse on the miller, his family, and the property they occupied.

Finally, trudging onward, she made her way to Paris, Maine, where she was greeted warmly and taken in by a young family with a sickly baby. They fed Molly and comforted her with warm blankets by the fire.

When she was rested she took the ailing infant in her arms, speaking quietly to him in her own language. She then told the mother that her child would not only recover, but would live to become an honorable and well-known dignitary with far-reaching fame.

The little boy, Hannibal Hamlin, grew up to become the twenty-third governor of Maine, six times a U.S. senator, minister to Spain, and ultimately the vigorously anti-slavery vice president of the United States under Abraham Lincoln.

Her prediction came true and so did her curse: The mill at Snow Falls burned to the ground. Over the years many businesses were attempted on that spot, but every one failed. In fact, nothing has flourished since Molly worked her magic there during that miserable winter night in 1809.

Molly Ockett died in Andover, Maine, and is buried there. Her tombstone reads:

MOLLOCKET

BAPTIZED

MARY AGATHA,

DIED IN THE CHRISTIAN FAITH,

AUGUST 2, A.D., 1816.

THE LAST OF THE PEQUAKETS.

## THE MYSTERY OF OLD TRICKEY

In this story it is difficult to determine who, or what, is cursed. There are several contenders: a town, a book, a man.

That there is a strong historical foundation to the tale cannot be questioned. "Old Trickey's" Bible exists, stowed away in the archives of the Old York Historical Society in Maine. I verified that fact after reading about it in a 1902 magazine article by Pauline Carrington Bouvé. The article says, "[Old Trickey's] bible, which is supposed to be haunted, is one of York's most cherished treasures."

Haunted?

Other accounts, equally ancient (1906), say the book is cursed.

But a cursed Bible? How can that be?

Apparently its curse is to remain forever closed. And the fact is, it won't stay open. As B. A. Botkin writes (1948), "[I]t will not stay opened, but flies back with a vicious snap; and some say they cannot push its black covers apart." In fact, it has been known to snap shut in people's hands.

Old Trickey—the original article explains—was "a piratical fisherman who lived at Bra'boat [Brave Boat] Harbor, [who] was very much feared along the coast as a malevolent creature who 'laid curses' on those he disliked."

Such a malignant specimen, you might surmise, would have little use for a Bible, so it would inevitably remain closed. That it insists on staying that way today suggests there is little chance for Old Trickey's redemption.

As I began to look into the story, I soon discovered that it is nearly impossible to separate grains of truth from grains of sand deposited by time's hourglass. And in this case there is a lot of sand to sort through.

Here's the tale, as best I can piece it together:

In about 1790 a stranger arrived in York, Maine, a former sea captain who appeared to be in his sixties. He said his name was Trickey. As we shall see, it may also have been his nature.

Townsfolk could learn very little about him. He was quiet, brooding, and, regardless of the situation, strangely reticent. He never spoke of a wife or children, and though he was obviously a sailor, he never mentioned his life at sea.

No one could have been more reclusive. He neither visited nor received neighbors. If he were to stop at the local tavern, he always sat and drank alone.

This solitary seaman might never have attracted any attention at all if disease had not broken out in the community. Something was wrong with the cattle, some vile contagion never before seen in the region. Incurable, lethal, and mysterious.

The next year large crops of flax failed when mold formed on their stalks. Corn mildewed. Sheep died in their pens.

People began to suspect there must be some relationship between their newest citizen and their developing misfortune.

Some men took it upon themselves to follow Old Trickey on his daily sojourns. Every day, it was discovered, the old man would walk into the woods and sit all by himself on a little knoll, where he'd remain for several hours.

Surely, they reasoned, he must be conjuring there. And sure enough, mishaps continued to befall the village. On the other hand, some thought, perhaps there was an alternate reason for solitary vigils. Since everyone "knew" he had been a pirate, if not a sorcerer, maybe he was out there guarding his buried treasure.

A group of locals worked up the courage to follow Captain Trickey with the intention of confronting him. While they trailed him, the afternoon clouded up and a bitter nor'easter blew in, as if to discourage further pursuit. Snow blew and blasted, but they persisted, making their way through the woods that separated them from the crashing sea. When they finally came upon Old Trickey at his observation post, they were aghast to discover he was stiff and dead. He looked like an ice statue, covered as he was with a frozen layer of snow.

When the storm ended they dug a hole and buried him. Some kept on digging holes, hoping to find the pirate treasure that never seemed to materialize.

Their treasure hunt was to be short-lived. As an old account from the *Portsmouth [New Hampshire] Chronicle* stated, "The spot is marked by many ledges and hollows—for every delving party has found it best to leave in sudden haste, owing to unexplained phenomena."

In the years to come, talk at the wayside tavern on Raynes Neck revealed more details about Old Trickey's methods of enchantment. Many admitted to having seen him in an odd pursuit: trying to bind quantities of sand with loops of rope. They speculated that was a conjuring technique: In order for Old Trickey's many curses to work, he'd had to tie up a certain amount of sand. Though it appeared a Sisyphean labor, it apparently got results, for the village suffered greatly under Old Trickey's tenure.

According to tradition, Trickey's death brought him, and the town, a reversal of fortune. Now and forever, the curse is on Captain Trickey. He is condemned to collect sand for all eternity. Amid the howls of a seaside gale an ominous voice can sometimes be heard to thunder, "More rope, more rope," as the sand sprays and swirls from York's dunes and beaches.

And some folks say that occasionally, as moonlight blinks through the black storm clouds, the figure of an old man with shaggy locks flying in the wind can be briefly glimpsed as he tries in vain to coil ropes around mounds of sand that quickly scatter.

## WINCHESTER'S WEAPONS

Sarah Winchester was cursed in New England.

She ran away, as far as the Pacific Ocean, until she could flee no farther, then spent the rest of her life trying to dodge the consequence of the fatal malediction.

The problem, strictly speaking, was not hers but that of her husband's father: Oliver Winchester, inventor of "the gun that won the West"—the Winchester rifle.

As the American Civil War began, the Winchester Repeating Arms Company of New Haven, Connecticut, began to acquire a nearly limitless fortune from government contracts.

The rifles it produced were responsible for the deaths of thousands of American Indians and Confederate soldiers.

Oliver's son, William Wirt Winchester, married the belle of New Haven, Miss Sarah Pardee, in September 1862. In July 1866 they had their first child, Annie, who soon died of marasmus, a horrible wasting disease. They were never to have another child.

Sarah's period of grieving brought her dangerously close to illness, possibly madness. As she began to recover, her husband came down with consumption, wasting away and finally dying in 1881.

Sarah was devastated. That she had inherited nearly $20 million, half of Winchester Arms, in addition to an income of $1,000 a day (that's about $18,000 a day in today's funds), gave her no relief; she was inconsolable.

Since psychiatric help was not available in those days, she—like so many others at the time—sought the help of a spiritualist. She consulted a respected Boston medium named Adam Coons, who told her there was a curse on her life, the result of the terrible weapon the Winchester family had created. The deaths of thousands of people were on her hands, and all were crying out for vengeance.

When she asked what she could do, the medium told her to go west, get as far away as possible, and build a house, not only for herself but for all those who had died by her weapon. "As long as you build," Adam Coons said, "you will live. Stop, and you will die."

It was then that Sarah Pardee Winchester sold all her Connecticut holdings and relocated to San Jose, California. There she commenced construction on one of the strangest architectural oddities ever built in this county. She hired a crew of carpenters who added room after room, day after day, working around the clock and never stopping.

The house grew to monstrous proportions, eventually reaching seven stories, containing a labyrinth of forty bedrooms, thirteen bathrooms, forty staircases (several of which lead nowhere), forty-seven fireplaces (four having flues that dead-end), half a dozen kitchens, two ballrooms, and, at the heart of the house, a séance room.

Many oddities, traps, and cul-de-sacs were built in to confuse malicious spirits. Among her bizarre castle's extreme peculiarities are a room with a window in the floor, doors that open onto blank walls, another door 8 feet above a kitchen sink, bathrooms with transparent glass walls, and more.

Although the building was damaged in the 1906 earthquake, construction continued until Sarah died in 1922 at age eighty-two. Even today it is impossible to get an exact count of the rooms because the place is so eccentrically laid out. Apparently there are more than 160 rooms covering over four and a half acres.

Presumably the curse ended with Sarah Winchester's death, but the house lives on, perhaps taking its life from the many souls that followed her there and are now trapped inside. The Winchester Mystery House, as it is now called, is reputed to be one of the most haunted houses in the country.

## CHAMPLAIN CURSE

There are many stories of the cursed ships that have sailed New England coastal waters. But it is rare to find a jinxed vessel on an inland lake.

One of particular interest to me is an allegedly cursed ship associated with Lake Champlain. I'm referring to the *Oakes Ames*, perhaps the largest, most powerful steamboat ever to sail those waters. It was built in 1868 in a Burlington shipyard, where it was christened in honor of the famous Massachusetts congressman.

The *Oakes Ames* was 258 feet long axnd 35 feet wide. Its paddle-wheel housings and twin 270-horsepower engines could push the behemoth along at 19 miles per hour. The *Oakes Ames* was designed to transport railroad cars. For six successful years, making four round trips a day, it ferried trains between Burlington, Vermont, and Plattsburgh, New York, a kind of traveling railroad bridge. But circa 1873 a reconfiguration of rail service on the New York side made this car ferry obsolete.

In 1874 the Champlain Transportation Company purchased the *Oakes Ames* and converted it into a plush passenger ferry.

But an ill-advised part of the conversion process was to rename the ship. Among seasoned salts it is well known that you *never* tamper with the name of a vessel. If you change a ship's name, you change its luck. And until now, the *Oakes Ames* had been a lucky ship.

But company policy overrode nautical wisdom. The practice was to name all vessels after geographic features of the lake. In addition, Congressman Ames had fallen from grace as a major perpetrator of the so-called Crédit Mobilier scandal, perhaps the biggest railroad-related financial scam in American history.

So the *Oakes Ames* became the *Champlain*. In effect, the company had cursed its own ship.

By the next year the twin railroad tracks and cavernous interior were gone, replaced by a richly carpeted grand hall and forty-one passenger staterooms. There was a fine restaurant aboard, a barbershop, even a post office.

All went well for the first ten days of operation.

Then, on July 16, at nine-thirty, on a clear, calm night with a full moon shining, the *Champlain* left Westport, New York, heading north with fifty-three passengers aboard. Most were asleep in their cabins.

Around midnight John Eldredge replaced Pilot Ell Rockwell at the wheel. Pilot Rockwell reported that Mr. Eldredge "appeared glum" and admitted that he wasn't feeling very well.

Just moments later, the ship suddenly rose up out of the water. As historian Don Wickman says, "The night's silence was broken by a resounding crash and the boat shuddered its entire length. No one knew what exactly had just happened." The purser, Abijah North, feared they had hit a canal boat and were shoving it farther down into the water.

Mr. Rockwell raced back to the pilothouse to find the *Champlain* rammed up onto the rocks of Steam Mill Point, its back broken by the severe impact. Mr. Eldredge appeared dazed, repeatedly asking, "Can you account for my being on the mountain?"

"You must have been asleep, John," Mr. Rockwell ventured.

"My God, how can that be? I was steering as I always steer, clear of the mountains . . ."

John Eldredge was never able to explain why he had run aground. He had twenty-three years of maritime experience and was familiar with every rock in the lake.

All the passengers were quickly rescued. Only two suffered minor injuries at the moment of impact. But the *Champlain* was doomed; it would never ply the lake again.

Its loss meant double misfortune for the Champlain Transportation Company. Not only did it lose its grandly refurbished steamboat, but it also lost a fortune: The ship was not insured against maritime disasters, only fire.

Still—according to certain students of sea lore—there is far more to the story. They point to another curse—a stronger curse—that overrides the simple renaming of a vessel.

The problem, they say, is in the name the Champlain Transportation Company picked; it could not have been more lethal. For disaster seems to follow any vessel called *Champlain*.

An earlier steamer on Lake Champlain was the first to bear the name of the lake. It was built in 1816 in Vergennes, Vermont, only to be destroyed by flames the following year. Ironically, it met its fiery end at Whitehall, New York, a town renowned as "the birthplace of the American Navy."

But the "Champlain Curse" doesn't confine itself to Lake Champlain. A steam side-wheeler called *Champlain* wrecked at Ste. Genevieve, Missouri, on the Mississippi River on December 11, 1834.

And in June 1875, a 1,473-ton sailing ship named *Champlain* wrecked off the coast of California.

Coincidence? Most likely. But among superstitious men of the sea, the Champlain Curse is well known, though its motive and its source—the original uttering—may be lost in the misty past.

We can only speculate that when Samuel de Champlain sailed down the lake in 1609, he brought with him the beginnings of a European intrusion that would change the continent forever. Is it any wonder that those whose lives were so dramatically and permanently altered—especially those with malevolent powers—would curse his name and all the boats that bear it?

## COLOR CURSES

A series of stories demonstrates how preternatural turbulence can leave its mark on the colors of nature. I refer to these phenomena as the "Color Curses," many examples of which can be found throughout New England.

For instance, up until the early twentieth century, the

Narragansett Indians told how "red-hearted spruce trees" grew anywhere a drop of Narragansett blood was spilled.

Another reminder of colonial brutality against the indigenous population comes from Maine. Near the oldest house on Chebeagne Island is a peculiar white moss that seems to grow there and nowhere else. For years it has eluded botanical classification. Its queerest attribute is that it turns blood red, but only for a single day each year. Is it curse or coincidence that an Indian massacre took place near that spot on the very day the moss's color changes?

Then there are the bloody rhododendrons that grow in Pine Swamp in Ledyard, Connecticut. Often referred to as the Curse of Cuppacommock, the story was told by the Stonington Pequots and recorded by Miss Polly Stoddard sometime in the late nineteenth century.

Because masts for ships were harvested there, Cuppacommock became known as Mast Swamp to the English. But it earned another reputation as well, for it was a place of retreat and refuge for the Pequot Indians. Here they could easily elude English invaders by darting among the twists of its labyrinthine trails, or hiding within its dark and inaccessible nooks and crannies.

The Curse of Cuppacommock came about after one Major Mason destroyed the Pequot stronghold at Mystic and pursued the few bedraggled remnants of the tribe—led by Puttaquapouk—into the swamp.

It was late June 1637, and the wild rhododendrons were just beginning to flower. One hundred twenty soldiers under Captain Stoughton of the Massachusetts Bay Colony surrounded the hiding fugitives. Some were captured as slaves; some were marched off and murdered.

Apparently Puttaquapouk's life was temporarily spared when he promised to help the English root out some of their other Indian "enemies." When he learned what his captors had done to his people, however, he would aid them no more.

The English led him into the swamp, tied him among the blossoming rhododendrons, took aim at his heart, and gave him one more chance to change his mind.

Instead, he declared the swamp's golden flowers would turn to blood as an eternal reminder of the Englishman's treachery.

The soldiers then pulled their triggers. Puttaquapouk died among the flowers that until that day had been golden, and forever after would bloom blood red.

An interesting footnote to the story is that if these much-desired Mast Swamp rhododendrons are uprooted and moved, the blossoms will lose their crimson brilliance and return to their traditional golden color.

They cannot be successfully transplanted from the swamp.

## MICAH ROOD

In 1699 Micah Rood settled in the Peck Hollow section of Franklin, a small town in eastern Connecticut. Though he was cheerful and friendly enough, he was not known as an ambitious man. He got by, but his farm never prospered.

Micah, like everyone else, eagerly took part in the excitement when the tin pan peddler came to town. These itinerant salesmen with their garish wagons and colorful patter were a welcome form of entertainment to the isolated inhabitants of early Yankee outposts such as Franklin. For housewives, the visiting businessman was a Santa Claus with a pack full of gaudy trinkets, along with more utilitarian items—like pots and pans—nowhere else available.

This particular peddler, Mr. Horgan, had a way of flattering the ladies while flashing semibawdy asides to the men. Part merchant, part scalawag, these mobile merchants have disappeared from the New England landscape.

And Peddler Horgan was about to disappear from Franklin, Connecticut.

He ended his presentation with the promise that he'd return to Franklin Green (then called Nine Mile Square) the very next day with a brand-new assortment of surprises. He then clattered off down the road to spend the night in some barn or shaded glen, for the likes of tin pan peddlers were not welcome at village inns.

When last seen, Mr. Horgan was headed out toward Peck Hollow.

The next day, however, he failed to reappear.

This was not cause for much concern, because the word of such rogues of the road was never very reliable. But disappointment turned to horror when, later that day, some boys discovered his lifeless body lying under an apple tree, his head split open by a heavy knife or ax, his inventory completely gone.

Peddler Horgan's corpse was found on the property owned by Micah Rood. Of course Micah was questioned about the homicide, but he claimed to know nothing of it. Though many suspected the farmer of the murder, there was absolutely no proof connecting him with the crime.

Yet after the horrifying event, two things happened. Micah Rood grew more taciturn and withdrawn by the year. But stranger still was the change to the apple tree under which Peddler Horgan's body was found. That next spring it began to blossom as usual. This year, however, for the first time, the lovely apple blossoms were crimson instead of their traditional white.

When the apples ripened they appeared exactly as they always had, but when a passing farmer picked one up and bit into it, he discovered a bloody red droplet near the apple's core.

Now townspeople believed not only that Micah Rood had murdered the peddler, but also that the peddler must have uttered a terrible curse before Micah delivered the death blow. Micah Rood's guilt would be forever displayed at the scene of the crime.

In the years that followed, Micah Rood neglected his farm, became more remote and withdrawn, and eventually descended to the status of town pauper. He died an invalid under the care of various overseers on December 17, 1728, and was buried at the town's expense.

But for the next 200 years, the apples (known locally as Mikes) from that tree—and that tree only—have continued to drip blood. So the story, and Micah Rood's apparent guilt, were not to be forgotten.

Then in 1938 the tree was uprooted by a hurricane. Although various attempts have been made to reproduce the sanguinary mikes (by planting seeds and grafting branches), the bloody apple tree—the only one of its kind ever known to exist—cannot be reproduced.

The validity of Micah Rood's guilt has never been proven, but the truth of his bloody apple tree has never been seriously questioned.

## RUTHLESS

There may be some disagreement among sports fans as to who is *America's* baseball team, but no one doubts the identity of *New England's* team—it's the Boston Red Sox.

In the early 1900s, when baseball was coming out of the pastures to become the country's All-American Sport, the Sox were the undisputed kings of the diamond. The team won five World Series, three of them rapid-fire in 1915, 1916, and 1918.

Then puppy love reared its ugly head.

Bosox owner Harry Frazee, needing money to finance his girlfriend's Broadway acting career, did the unthinkable. On January 3, 1920, he sold baseball's greatest star, George Herman "Babe" Ruth. Worse yet, he sold the Bambino to the hated New York Yankees. The price: a measly $125,000 (about $1,253,515 in today's dollars).

The Babe, it is said, was so upset by the deal, the rejection, and the relocation that on the train ride from Boston to New York he cursed his former team to make sure they would never win another World Series.

The Babe was always true to his word. In more than eighty years since then, they haven't.

During an interview, Red Sox historian Jim DeFilippi told me, "The Bambino's Curse is made even more ominous by the various heartbreaking ways the Sox have lost the championship. Four different times—in 1946, 1967, 1975, 1986—they went all the way to the seventh game, the deciding game of the World Series. Then they lost.

"In 1978 a three-run home run by normally weak-hitting Yankee infielder Bucky Dent accomplished the same thing," he said. "From that point on his sobriquet all over New England was Bucky F***in' Dent."

Then in 1986, just as fans began to believe the curse was all but dead, a slow-rolling ball eased its way between the legs of Boston first baseman Bill Buckner. Even a Little Leaguer should have been able to snag that grounder. The impossible error sent the Sox to the showers and won Buckner the stature of a New England anti-Christ.

When Ruth entered the lineup, the New York Yankees began their ascent, eventually becoming the greatest dynasty in sport's history, winning twenty-six World Series and often denying the Sox entry into the event.

In 2003 the Yanks hit an extra-innings walk-off home run that eliminated the Sox from World Series contention.

After eighty years, the Curse of the Bambino was finally broken in 2004 when the Red Sox pulled off an amazing come-from-behind victory against the Yankees in the American League Championship Series. The also won the World Series in 2007 and 2013. Though the Red Sox seem to have broken their curse, they—along with their fans—continue to regard the New York team as "the Damned Yankees."

# APPENDIX

## A PORTION OF AN ANGLICAN "COMMINATION SERVICE"

*Priest:* Cursed is the man that maketh any carved or molten image, to worship it. And the people shall answer and say: Amen.

*Priest:* Cursed is he that curseth his father or mother.

*Answer:* Amen.

*Priest:* Cursed is he that removeth his neighbour's landmark.

*Answer:* Amen.

*Priest:* Cursed is he that maketh the blind to go out of his way.

*Answer:* Amen.

*Priest:* Cursed is he that perverteth the judgement of the stranger, the fatherless, and widow.

*Answer:* Amen.

*Priest:* Cursed is he that smiteth his neighbour secretly.

*Answer:* Amen.

*Priest:* Cursed is he that lieth with his neighbour's wife.

*Answer:* Amen.

*Priest:* Cursed is he that taketh reward to slay the innocent.

*Answer:* Amen.

*Priest:* Cursed is he that putteth his trust in man, and taketh man for his defence, and in his heart goeth from the Lord.

*Answer:* Amen.

*Priest:* Cursed are the unmerciful, fornicators, and adulterers, covetous persons, idolaters, slanderers, drunkards, and extortioners.

*Answer:* Amen.

# SOURCES

## DAMNED YANKEES

Boyer, Paul, and Stephen Nissenbaum. *Salem Possessed* (Cambridge, Mass.: Harvard University Press, 1974).

Cahill, Robert Ellis. *Strange Superstitions* (Salem, Mass.: Old Saltbox Publishing, 1990).

Citro, Joseph A. *Green Mountain Ghosts* (Boston: Houghton Mifflin, 1994).

Citro, Joseph A., and Diane E. Foulds. *Curious New England* (Hanover, NH.: University Press of New England, 2003).

Godwin, David F. "Curses!" (Lakeville, N.M.: *Fate Magazine*, March 2001).

Hall, David D. *Worlds of Wonder, Days of Judgment* (Cambridge, Mass.: Harvard University Press, 1989).

Hill, Frances. *A Delusion of Satan* (New York: Doubleday, 1995).

Karlson, Carol F. *The Devil in the Shape of a Woman* (New York: W. W. Norton, 1987).

Koehler, Lyle. *A Search for Power* (Chicago: University of Illinois Press, 1980).

Mills, Cynthia. "Dying Well in Montpelier: The Story of the Hubbard Memorial" (Montpelier, Vt.: *Vermont History Magazine*, Winter–Spring 2000).

Sieveking, Paul. "Nothing but Trouble" (Westport, Conn.: *Mysteries of Mind, Space & Time,* 13, H. S. Stuttman, 1992).

"A DREADFUL WIZARD"

Boyer, Paul, and Stephen Nissenbaum. *Salem Possessed* (Cambridge, Mass.: Harvard University Press, 1974).

Cahill, Robert Ellis. *Haunted Happenings* (Salem, Mass.: Old Saltbox Publishing, 1992).

———. *New England's Witches and Wizards* (Peabody, Mass.: Chandler-Smith Publishing, 1983).

Drake, Samuel Adams. *New England Legends and Folk Lore* (Boston: Roberts Brothers, 1884).

MacIver, Kenneth, and William Thomson. *Tales for a New England Night* (Cape Neddick, Maine: Nor'East Heritage Publications, 1980).

Norton, Mary Beth. *In the Devil's Snare* (New York: Knopf, 2002).

THE BURTON AIL

Beals, Charles Edward, Jr. (William James Sidis). *Passaconaway in the White Mountains* (Boston: Badger, 1916).

Bolte, Mary, and Mary Eastman. *Haunted New England* (New York: Weathervane Books, 1972).

Cushing, Carol. *Longstreet Highroad Guide to the New Hampshire Mountains* (Atlanta: Longstreet Press, 1999).

Drake, Samuel Adams. *Heart of the White Mountains* (New York: Harper & Brothers, 1882).

Fox, Charles J., and Samuel Osgood, eds. *The New Hampshire Book* (Nashua, N.H.: David Marshall, 1842).

Kilbourne, Frederick W. *Chronicles of the White Mountains* (Boston: Houghton Mifflin, 1916).

Merrill, Georgia Drew. *History of Carroll County.* Facsilime of the 1889 edition (Somersworth, N.H.: Somersworth Publishing, 1971).

Mudge, John T. B. *The White Mountains: Names, Places & Legends* (Etna, N.H.: Durand Press, 1992, 1995).

Norris, Curt. *The Man Who Talked to Trees* (North Attleboro, Mass.: Covered Bridge Press, 1996).

Speare, Eva A., ed. *New Hampshire Folk Tales* (Canaan, N.H.: Phoenix Publishing, 1945, 1974).

## THE SAGA OF THE SACO RIVER

Beaupré, Normand. *Lumineau* (Quebec: Lees éditions JCL, 2002).

Goodman, Giselle. "Beautiful but Cruel, The Saco Reveals Her Many Moods" (*Blethen Maine Newspapers*, August 14, 2002).

Hallett, Richard. "Saco River Outlives Indian Curse" (Portland, Maine: *Sunday Telegram*, June 29, 1947).

"Saco River Bears an Old Curse Which Has Been Fulfilled Yearly Since 1675" (Portland, Maine: *Sunday Telegram*, July 26, 1931).

Verde, Thomas A. *Maine Ghosts and Legends* (Camden, Maine: Down East Books, 1989).

York, Dane. *History of Biddeford* (City of Biddeford, Maine, year unknown).

## A BLIGHTED CAMPAIGN

Bassett, T. D. Seymour. *Outsiders Inside Vermont* (Brattleboro, Vt.: Stephen Greene Press, 1967).

Calloway, Colin G. *The Western Abenakis of Vermont, 1600–1800* (Norman, Okla.: University of Oklahoma Press, 1990).

Citro, Joseph A. *Green Mountain Ghosts* (Boston: Houghton Mifflin, 1994).

Drake, Samuel Adams. *New England Legends* (Boston: Roberts Company, 1884).

Duffy, John. *Vermont, an Illustrated History* (Northridge, Calif.: Windsor Publications, 1985).

Grow, Margarite. *Stories of Old Bradford* (Privately published, 1955).

Haskins, Harold W. *A History of Bradford* (Littleton, N.H.: Courier Printing, 1968).

Hill, Ralph Nading. *Yankee Kingdom* (New York: Harper & Brothers, 1960).

———. *Lake Champlain: Key to Liberty* (Montpelier, Vt.: *Vermont Life*, 1976).

Jameson, W. C. *Buried Treasures of New England* (Little Rock, Ark.: August House, 1998).

Leduc, Gérard. Personal correspondence, March 2002.

Pike, Robert. *Drama on the Connecticut* (New Jersey: H-H Press, 1975).

Roberts, Kenneth. *Northwest Passage* (Garden City, N.Y.: Doubleday, Doran, 1937).

Saunderson, Rev. Henry H. *History of Charlestown, New Hampshire* (1876).

Spaulding, John H. *Guide and Historical Relics of the White Mountains* (Mount Washington, N.H.: J. R. Hitchcock, 1862).

## THE PHANTOM FOOT

Citro, Joseph A., and Diane E. Foulds. *Curious New England* (Hanover, N.H.: University Press of New England, 2003).

Coffin, Robert P. Tristram. *Collected Poems of . . .* (New York: Macmillan, 1948).

Eastman, Mary, and Mary Bolte. *Haunted New England* (New York: Weathervane Books, 1972).

Roadside America Web site, http://roadsideamerica.com.

Sample, Tim, and Steve Bither. *Maine Curiosities* (Guilford, Conn.: The Globe Pequot Press, 2002).

Timmons, Karen. "Ghost Hunters Find Rich Harvest in USA" (Bridgeport, Conn.: *Sunday Post,* November 2, 1986).

Verde, Thomas A. *Maine Ghosts and Legends* (Camden, Maine: Down East Books, 1989).

## THE MISSING MAN

Drake, Samuel Adams. *New England Legends and Folk Lore* (Boston: Roberts Brothers, 1884).

Frank, Frederick S. *Through the Pale Door* (Westport, Conn.: Greenwood Press, 1990).

Hawthorne, Nathaniel. "A Virtuoso's Collection." In *Mosses from an Old Manse*, 1846.

———. "Ethan Brand." In *The Snow-Image, and Other Twice-told Tales*, 1850.

Nadler, Holly Mascott. *Ghosts of Boston Town* (Camden, Maine: Down East Books, 2002).

Snow, Edward Rowe. *Fantastic Folklore and Fact* (New York: Dodd, Mead, 1968).

Stevens, Austin N., ed. *Mysterious New England* (Dublin, N.H.: Yankee, Inc., 1971).

Terramorsi, Bernard. "'Peter Rugg, the Missing Man' or The Eclipsing Revolution: an Essay on the Supernatural." Translated by Alain Geoffroy (Saint Denis, France: Université de La Réunion, Faculté des Lettres & Sciences Humaines, March 1996).

CONNECTICUT'S VILLAGE
OF THE DAMNED

Cahill, Robert Ellis. *New England's Ghostly Haunts* (Peabody, Mass.: Chandler-Smith Publishing, 1983).

Chamberlain, Paul H. *Dudleytown* (Cornwall, Conn.: Cornwall Historical Society, 1966).

Citro, Joseph A. *Passing Strange: True Tales of New England Hauntings and Horrors* (Boston: Houghton Mifflin, 1996).

Clark, Harriet Lydia. *True Facts About Dudleytown* (Cornwall, Conn.: Cornwall Historical Society, 1989).

———. "Descendant Demystifies Dudleytown" (Litchfield, Conn.: *County News*, October 25, 1985).

Dudley, Gary P. *The Legend of Dudleytown: Solving Legends Through Genealogical and Historical Research* (Westminster, Md.: Heritage Books, 2001). Rev. Gary Dudley of Texas, a distant member of the Dudley line, has done the most thorough investigation of Dudleytown to date. For those interested in the facts as well as the fantasies, I recommend his book—the only one completely devoted to Dudleytown.

Philips, David E. *Legendary Connecticut* (Willimantic, Conn.: Curbstone Press, 1992).

Sheff, David. "Playboy Interview: Dan Aykroyd" (*Playboy*, August 1993).

Sterry, Iveagh, and William Garrigus. *They Found a Way* (Brattleboro, Vt.: Stephen Daye Press, 1938).

Stevens, Austin N. *Mysterious New England* (Dublin, N.H.: Yankee, Inc., 1971).

Warren, Ed and Lorraine. *Ghost Hunters* (New York: St. Martins Press, 1989).

Winkler, Robert. "Birder's Journal: Old Curse Haunts New England Forest" (*National Geographic News*, October 30, 2002).

Yeadon, David. *Hidden Corners of New England* (New York: Funk & Wagnalls, 1976).

## NIX'S MATE

Boston Harbor Islands: pamphlets published by Boston Harbor Islands Partnership.

Cahill, Robert Ellis. *New England's Things That Go Bump in the Night* (Peabody, Mass.: Chandler-Smith Publishing, 1989).

Dorson, Richard. *Jonathan Draws the Long Bow* (Cambridge, Mass.: Harvard University Press, 1946).

Drake, Samuel Adams. *New England Legends and Folk Lore* (Boston: Roberts Brothers, 1884).

Snow, Edward R. *The Islands of Boston Harbor* (New York: Dodd, Mead, 1936, 1971).

Stevens, Austin N., ed. *Mysterious New England* (Dublin, N.H.: Yankee, Inc., 1971).

## THAT OLD SAND FARM

Citro, Joseph A., and Diane E. Foulds. *Curious New England* (Lebanon, N.H.: University Press of New England, 2003).

Desert of Maine promotional brochures.

Sample, Tim, and Steve Bither. *Maine Curiosities* (Guilford, Conn.: The Globe Pequot Press, 2002).

Schulte, Carol Olivieri. *Ghosts on the Coast of Maine* (Camden, Maine: Down East Books, 1989).

Thomas, Randall, director, Freeport Maine Historical Society. E-mail correspondence and telephone interview, March 7, 2003, March 12, 2003, and March 26, 2003.

## NO MERCY FROM MERCIE DALE

Citro, Joseph A. *Green Mountain Ghosts* (Boston: Houghton Mifflin, 1994).

Hard, Walter R., Jr., and Janet C. Greene, eds. *Mischief in the Mountains* (Montpelier, Vt.: *Vermont Life*, 1970).

Harriman, Lottie G. Rogers. "Friendship and a Curse" (Green Mountain Folklore Society: *Green Mountain Whittlin's* XXVI, Fall 1974).

Hemenway, Abby Maria, ed. *Vermont Historical Gazetteer* (Burlington, Vt.: 1868-1891).

Lamoureux, Louis A. "Fall of the House of Hayden" (Montpelier, Vt.: *Vermont Life*, Fall 1964).

Lawrence, David. *This Is Albany* (Albany, Vt.: Privately published, 1976).

Warton, Virginia, ed. *History of Albany, Vermont, 1806–1991* (Albany, Vt.:, 1991). See particularly "The Chadwick Family" by Evelyn Heath Chadwick (pp. 95–97) and "Something of the House of Hayden" by Iola Wallace Wylie (pp. 167–71).

## FATE AND THE *PHOENIX*

Hemenway, Abby Maria, ed. *Vermont Historical Gazetteer* (Burlington, Vt.: 1867).

Hill, Ralph Nading. *Lake Champlain: Key to Liberty* (Montpelier, Vt.: *Vermont Life*, 1976).

Kane, Adam, Archaeologist, Lake Champlain Maritime Museum. Personal interview, February 6, 2003.

Sedgwick, Theodore. *Hints to My Countrymen* (New York: J. Seymour, Printer, 1826).

Zarzynski, Joseph W. *Monster Wrecks of Loch Ness and Lake Champlain* (Wilton, N.Y.: M-Z Information, 1986).

## THE WITCH AND THE VIRGIN

Butler, Caleb. *History of the Town of Groton, Including Pepperell and Shirley, from the First Grant of Groton Plantation in 1655* (1848).

Chase, Jacqueline R. "Curse of North Pepperell Recalled in The Deserted Village' by Teacher" (Lowell, Mass.: *Lowell Sun*, July 11, 1958).

Citro, Joseph A., and Diane E. Foulds. *Curious New England* (Hanover, N.H.: University Press of New England, 2003).

Flight, Wilson R., ed. *A Pepperell Reader* (Pepperell, Mass., Historical Society, 1975).

Healy, Monica. "Prophecy of the Witch" (Pepperell, Mass.: *Times Free Press*, January 21, 1987).

Ramsey, Sybil. "The Deserted Village" (1923). In an undated document from the Lawrence Library, Pepperell, Mass.

Robbins, Lyman F. "A History of Pepperell" (East Pepperell, Mass.: *Times-Free Press*, July 3, 1969).

Sibley, Florence G. "The Witch's Prophecy" (Lawrence Library archives, Pepperell, Mass., 1910).

Song, Debbie. "The Tenacity of Superstition: The Pepperell Witch Tale" (Pepperell, Mass.: *Times Free Press*, January 21, 1987, and January 28, 1987).

Unknown. "Witch's Curse: Did It Ravage Pepperell Village More than a Century Ago?" (Pepperell Library, unidentified newspaper dated July 23, year unknown).

Willard, Mabel. "No One Shall Live in This Town" (Dublin, N.H.: *Yankee Magazine*, November 1971).

## THE TREE OF KNOWLEDGE

Davis, Karen L. "Duxbury Communitywide Survey—Phase I" (Duxbury, Mass., Historical Commission, July 3, 2001).

"Duxbury's Tree of Knowledge Has Long Been A Landmark" (Duxbury, Mass.: Duxbury *Clipper*, November 11, 1951).

Fish, Henry A. "Duxbury, Massachusetts, Ancient and Modern: A Sketch, with Map and Key" (Binghamton, N.Y., 1924).

Gallant, Frank K. *A Place Called Peculiar* (Springfield, Mass.: Merriam-Webster, 1998).

Norris, Lowell Ames. "Duxbury Uneasy with Sign Gone from Site of 'Tree of Knowledge'" (*Boston Herald*, August 26, 1923).

Peterson, Reuben, M.D. "The Tree of Knowledge" (Plymouth, Mass.: The Old Colony Memorial, July 1, 1937).

Pillsbury, Katherine H. *Duxbury, A Guide* (Duxury, Mass.: Duxbury Rural & Historical Society, 1999).

"Tree of Knowledge" (Duxbury, Mass.: Duxbury *Clipper*, February 17, 1955).

Winsor, Justin. "History of the Town of Duxbury, Massachusetts, with Genealogical Registers" (Boston: Crosby & Nichols, 1849).

## AN IDOL REVENGE

Citro, Joseph A., and Diane E. Foulds. *Curious New England* (Hanover, N.H.: University Press of New England, 2003).

Dingle, Robert J. *Story of Naples* (Naples, Maine, Historical Society, 1979).

Ferriss, Lloyd. Article. *Maine Sunday Telegram* (November 29, 1987).

Naples, Maine, Historical Society. Interviews and materials.

Verde, Thomas A. *Maine Ghosts and Legends* (Camden, Maine: Down East Books, 1989).

## HAUNTED WATERS

Alexande, Elleen. "Townspeople O.K. purchase of the Brunswick Springs" (Lancaster, N.H.: *Coos County Democrat*, September 16, 1992).

——. "Abenakis Purchase Historic Brunswick Springs Site" (Lancaster, N.H.: *Coos County Democrat*, December 16, 1992).

Chapman, Randolph W. *The Origin of Brunswick Springs, Vermont* (*Marshall Review* 1, no. 3, March 1938).

Citro, Joseph A. *Green Mountain Ghosts* (Boston: Houghton Mifflin, 1994).

Crosier, Barney. "Brunswick Springs—Bedeviled Waters of the Great Spirit" (Rutland, Vt.: *Sunday Herald* and *Times Argus*, September 8, 1985).

Hunter, Verne M., and Majorie M. Carrier. *History of Brunswick Vermont* (Town of Brunswick, Vt., 1977).

Joos, Dennis. "Fire and Water" (Montpelier, Vt.: *Vermont Life,* Summer 1984).

Jordan, Charles J. *Tales Told in the Shadows of the White Mountains* (Lebanon, N.H.: University Press of New England, 2003).

Matson, Tim. *Round-Trip to Deadsville* (White River Junction, Vt.: Chelsea Green, 2000).

## A SHADOW OVER CROMPTON

Carpenter, Donald. Personal interview, September 29, 2003.

Carrier, Aimee. "Does Crompton Have Its Own Ghost?" (Kent County, R.I.: *Daily Times,* undated).

Federal Writer's Project. Rhode Island: *A Guide to the Smallest State* (Boston: Houghton Mifflin, 1937).

Fitzgerald, Fr. Edmund H., Ph.D. "The Ghost of Mrs. Mary (Hodson) Doran." Signed affidavit dated August 19, 2002.

———. Personal interview, September 29, 2003.

Hughes, Richard. Personal interview, September 28, 2003.

Pawtuxet Valley Preservation and Historical Society Web site, www.geocities.com/pvphs2000.

Plante, Normand. Pawtuxet Valley Preservation and Historical Society. Personal correspondence and interview, August 7, 2003.

## THE CRASH OF CAMELOT

Collier, Peter, and David Horowitz. *The Kennedys: An American Drama* (San Francisco: Encounter Books, 2001).

Hamilton, Edith. *Mythology* (Boston: Little, Brown and Co., 1942).

Hamilton, Nigel. *JFK: Reckless Youth* (New York: Random House, 1992).

Kessler, Ronald. *The Sins of the Father* (New York: Warner Books, 1996).

Klein, Edward. *The Kennedy Curse* (New York: St. Martin's Press, 2003).

——. Interview on CBS News, July 9, 2003.

Leamer, Laurence. *The Kennedy Men* (New York: William Morrow, 2001).

Reeves, Richard. "JFK Secrets and Lies" (*Reader's Digest Magazine*, April 2003).

Smith, Amanda, ed. *Hostage to Fortune: The Letters of Joseph P. Kennedy* (New York: Viking, 2001).

~

A CLUSTER OF CURSES

**Lithobolia**

Burr, George L., ed. *Narratives of the Witchcraft Cases* (New York: Charles Scribner's Sons, 1914).

Citro, Joseph A. *Passing Strange: True Tales of New England Hauntings and Horrors* (Boston: Houghton Mifflin, 1996).

Drake, Samuel Adams. *New England Legends and Folk Lore* (Boston: Roberts Brothers, 1884).

**Molly Ockett**

Grumet, Robert S., ed. *Northeastern Indian Lives 1632–1816* (Amherst, Mass.: University of Massachusets Press, 1996).

Haldan, Dr. Robert, Jr. *Room For The Indians* (http://members.cox .net/fj.publications/RoomMain.htm).

Lecompte, Nancy. "The Last of the Androscoggins, Molly Ockett, Abenaki Healing Woman" (www.avcnet.org/ne-do -ba/bio_moly.html).

Tufts, Henry. "Life with the Abenaki in 1772" (www.avcnet .org/ne-do-ba/menh_tuf.shtml).

**The Mystery of Old Trickey**

Botkin, B. A. *A Treasury of New England Folklore* (New York: Bonanza Books, 1965).

Bouvé, Pauline Carrington. "Old York, A Forgotten Seaport" (*Scribner's Magazine*, 1902). Reprinted in *Tales of the New England Coast* (Secaucus, N.J.: Castle Books, 1985).

Brighto, Ray. "Capt. Trickey and Raynes' Neck" (*Portsmouth [N.H.] Herald*, December 4, 1988).

Norman, Michael, and Beth Scott. *Haunted Historic America* (New York: Tor Books, 1984).

Spiller, Virginia S. Librarian, Old York, Maine, Historical Society. Phone calls and personal correspondence, January 2003 and February 2003.

Sylvester, Herbert Milton. *Maine Pioneer Settlements: Old York* (Boston: W. B. Clarke Co., 1909).

**Winchester's Weapons**
Myers, Arthur. *The Ghostly Register* (New York: Dorset, 1986).

Stevens, Austin N. *Mysterious New England* (Dublin, N.H.: Yankee, Inc., 1971).

Winer, Richard, and Nancy Osborn. *Haunted Houses* (New York: Bantam Books, 1979).

**Champlain Curse**
Beck, Horace. *Folklore of the Sea* (Edison, N.J.: Castle Books, 1999).

Hill, Ralph Nading. *Lake Champlain Key to Liberty* (Montpelier, Vt.: *Vermont Life*, 1976).

Lane, Carl D. *American Paddle Steamboats* (New York: Coward-McCann, Inc., 1943).

Martin, Edward Winslow. *Behind the Scenes in Washington* (New York: Continental Publishing Company, 1873).

Wickman, Don. "Disaster on Lake Champlain" (Rutland, Vt., *Herald*, July 14, 2000).

Zarzynski, Joseph W. *Monster Wrecks of Loch Ness and Lake Champlain* (Wilton, N.Y.: M-Z Information, 1986).

**Color Curses**
Bolte, Mary, and Mary Eastman. *Haunted New England* (New York: Weathervane Books, 1972).

Dorson, Richard. *Jonathan Draws the Long Bow* (Cambridge, Mass.: Harvard University Press, 1946).

Hauptman, Laurence M., and James D. Wherry. *The Pequots in Southern New England* (Norman, Okla.: University of Oklahoma Press, 1990).

Skinner, Charles M. *American Myths and Legends* (Philadelphia and London: Lippincott, 1903).

**Micah Rood**
Philips, David E. *Legendary Connecticut* (Willimantic, Conn.: Curbstone Press, 1992).

Stevens, Austin N. *Mysterious New England* (Dublin, N.H.: Yankee, Inc., 1971).

**Ruthless**
DeFilippi, James. Personal interview, October 13, 2003.

# ACKNOWLEDGMENTS

I am indebted to a number of people for helping me put this cursed tome together. Here is a partial list. Some have requested anonymity. Others are omitted due to my Swiss cheese of a memory. My apologies to anyone I have inadvertently left out. My thanks to everyone. May you all be free of curses forever: Chris Avila, Normand Beaupré, Steve Bissette, Patrick Browne (director of the Duxbury, Massachusetts, Rural & Historical Society), Bob Cahill (former high sheriff of Salem, Massachusetts), Evelyn Chadwick, Sandy Chadwick, Brian and Allison Citro, Nancy Hayes Clune, Jim DeFilippi, Paul Eno, Diane E. Foulds, Chad Graham, Paul Grzybowski, Zeke Hanzel, Helen Husher, Charlie and Donna Jordan, Adam Kane, John Moody, Mary Norris, Valerie Osborne, Jeanne Palmer, Virginia S. Spiller (of the Old York Historical Society), Amber Sulick, and Ms. Randall Thomas (director of the Freeport Maine Historical Society).

A special thank-you to Jim Jaquette, assistant director of the Duxbury Free Library; and to Michael Bell, Rhode Island's favorite vampire hunter, for directing me to Normand Plante (not a vampire) of the Pawtuxet Valley Preservation and Historical Society, who then led me to Richard Hughes, Donald Carpenter, and the very helpful Fr. Edmund H. Fitzgerald, Ph.D.

Lastly, thank you to Jan Cronan at Globe Pequot Press who helped make this book possible.

# INDEX

## A

Albany, New Hampshire, 35
Albany, Vermont, 113, 118, 119, 125, 126
Andover, Maine, 219, 220

## B

Belvue Terrace, 164, 167
Black Agnes, 3–6
Black, Ida, 62
Boston, Massachusetts, 69, 73, 74
Boston Red Sox. *See* Red Sox
Bradley, Benjamin, 52–53, 58–59
Brunswick Spring House, 175
Brunswick Springs Hotel, 178–80, 181
Brunswick Springs, Vermont, 171–88
Buck, Col. Jonathan, 61–67
Bucksport, Maine, 61
Burton, New Hampshire, 28, 34, 35. *See also* Albany, New Hampshire

## C

Campbell, Cornelius, 28–35
*Champlain*, 226–28
Champlain, Lake, 127–34, 136, 225–28
Charlestown, Massachusetts, 76
Chebeagne Island, Maine, 229
Chief Chocorua. *See* Chocorua, Chief
Chief Squando. *See* Squando, Chief
Chocorua, Chief, 28–36

Concord, Massachusetts, 69, 74
Coons, Adam, 224
Corey, Giles, 16–22, 23, 24, 25
Cornwall, Connecticut, 86, 90. *See also* Dudleytown,
  Connecticut
Corwin, Sheriff George, 19–22, 23, 24
Craftsbury, Vermont, 114
Crompton, Rhode Island, 189, 190–91. *See also* West Warwick,
  Rhode Island
Cutter, Tom, 70–73, 77

D

Dale, Mercie, 114, 115–17
Dale, Silence, 113. *See also* Hayden, Silence
Desert of Maine, 107, 111, 112
Doran, Mary, 191–94, 195, 196, 197
Dudleytown, Connecticut, 83–98
Dunnellen Hall, 12–13
Duxbury, Massachusetts, 153–60

F

Franklin, Connecticut, 230
Freeport, Maine, 107

G

Good, Sarah, 10–11
Grayson, Hattie, 108–9
Greenwich, Connecticut, 12

H

Harraway, Ann. *See* Black, Ida
Hartford, Connecticut, 75

Hayden, Silence, 114, 117, 118–19
Hayden, William, 113–18
Hayden, William "Will," Jr., 118–23, 125–26
Hayloft, The, 167–68
Hill, Charles, 162–65
Hill, Ruben, 162–65
Horgan, Peddler, 230–32
Hutchins, John Corbin, 177–80, 181

J

Jacobson, Rabbi Israel, 204, 211

K

Kennedy, John Fitzgerald "Jack," 204, 205, 206–9
Kennedy, Joseph Patrick "Joe," 199–204, 205, 207, 213
Kennedy, Joseph Patrick "Joe Jr.," 204, 205–6
Kennedy, Robert Francis "Bobby," 209, 213
Kennedy, Ted, 209, 210, 213

L

Lake Champlain. See Champlain, Lake
Ledyard, Connecticut, 229
Lovejoy, Mistress, 140–43, 146, 147, 148
Lutterloh, Vermont, 114. See also Albany, Vermont

M

Marblehead, Massachusetts, 8
Marie Agatha. See Ockett, Molly
Menotomy, Massachusetts. See West Cambridge,
    Massachusetts
Montpelier, Vermont, 4, 6

# N

Naples, Maine, 161–62
Newburyport, Massachusetts, 76
Nickles, Rev. Samuel, 77–78
Nix's Mate Island, Massachusetts, 103–5
North Pepperell, Massachusetts, 137, 140–44, 147–49. *See also* Pepperell, Massachusetts
North Pepperell Witch, 140–43, 148
Noyes, Rev. Nicholas, 11

# O

Ockett, Molly, 218–20
Odanak. *See* St. Francis, Canada
"Old Trickery," 220–23
Old York, Maine, 220

# P

Paris, Maine, 219
Pepperell, Massachusetts, 137, 147, 150–51
*Phoenix*, 127–136
Pine Crest Lodge, 175
Portsmouth, New Hampshire, 215
Puttaquapouk, 229–30

# Q

Quonset, Rhode Island, 77

# R

Red Sox, 232–34
Reed, Wilmot "Mammy," 8
Rogers's Rangers, 48–60
Rood, Micah, 230–32

Rugg, Peter, 69–82
Ruth, George Herman "Babe," 233

S

Saco River, 37–45
Salem, Massachusetts, 10–11, 15–25
Serenity Hill, 168–69
Sherman, Capt. Jehaziel, 129, 134–35, 136
Sherman, Richard, 129, 130, 131, 135
Simms, Goody, 8
Singing Bird. See Ockett, Molly
Squando, Chief, 38–44
St. Francis, Canada, 47–48, 50, 59, 60
St. Mary's Catholic Church (Crompton, Rhode Island), 194–97
Sutton, Massachusetts, 9–10

T

Tarklin, Massachusetts. See Duxbury, Massachusetts
Tree of Knowledge, 153–60
Trickery, Captain. See "Old Trickery"

W

Wakefield, Goody, 9–10
Walton, George, 215–16
Waterville, Maine, 113, 124
West Cambridge, Massachusetts, 70
West Warwick, Rhode Island, 190
Wickford, Rhode Island, 77
Winchester Mystery House, 224–25
Winchester, Sarah Pardee, 223–24

Y

York, Maine, 221

# ABOUT THE AUTHOR

Known alternately as "Vermont's Ghostmaster General" and "New England's Bard of the Bizarre," Joseph A. Citro is doing more than anyone else to keep the region's legends and lore alive in popular culture. His books include five novels of suspense, three volumes of historical oddities, a collection of regional humor, and a travel guide. His best-selling *Green Mountain Ghosts, Ghouls and Unsolved Mysteries* (Houghton Mifflin, 1994) is the most comprehensive compilation of offbeat Vermontiana ever assembled (now in its tenth printing). It was supplemented by *Passing Strange* (1996), *Green Mountains, Dark Tales* (1999), and *The Vermont Ghost Guide* (2000). His novels—three of which have been optioned for motion pictures—present a dark and mystical side of the Vermont experience: *Shadow Child, Guardian Angels, The Gore, Lake Monsters,* and *Deus-X.* A native of Chester, Vermont, Joe has taught in local colleges, lectured widely, and appeared on regional and national radio and television. His Vermont Public Radio commentary series is heard regularly in five states and Canada. Two videos based on his Vermont oddities are currently in the works.

Learn more about Joe Citro's books at www.josephacitro.blogspot.com.

# ABOUT THE ILLUSTRATOR

Jeff White has illustrated several books as well as horror stories and comics, and he has created spot illustrations for magazines. Born in Southampton, New York, he has lived in New York, Tokyo, and Boston. He currently resides in Everett, Massachusetts, with his wife and two dogs.

CPSIA information can be obtained
at www.ICGtesting.com
Printed in the USA
BVHW051714240223
659183BV00014B/659